The Origins of Life

Sex Education in the Family

Mariele Quartana

new city press, new york

Published in the United States of America
by New City Press, the Publishing House of the
Focolare Movement, Inc., 206 Skillman Avenue,
Brooklyn, N.Y. 11211
© 1983, New City Press, Brooklyn, N.Y.
Printed in the United States of America
ISBN 0-911782-42-7
Library of Congress Catalog Card Number 82-60619

Translated from the original Italian Edition
La Verità sull'Origine della Vita, Città Nuova, Rome,
by New City Press

Cover photo: Meinolf Otto

CONTENTS

PREFACE

Children have the right to know how they came into the world. And, therefore, this must be explained to them. Even if educators were not always fully aware of it, this subject has always been of great importance; and it is becoming even more important for various reasons. The first of these is the trend in education that seeks to liberate both the educational system and those being educated from so-called taboos, in order that children may go through life free of complexes and inhibitions.

A second factor is the negative tendency in modern society to exploit the physical aspect of sex in films, publications and advertising and to consider it the main interest in human life.

Therefore, it is clear that parents who wish to raise their children in a complete and balanced way, free of hang-ups, but with a respect for sex, will have to make some effort to face and resolve this very real issue.

In the last few years, there have been many publications aimed at helping mothers and fathers explain how life begins. Some of these are really excellent; they are thorough and complete. So rather than try to compete with these, we would like to present a series of interviews as a help to the many parents who have expressed a need for some practical examples drawn from actual experiences of fathers and mothers like themselves. We have already tried this approach in relaxed and informal meetings with individuals and with groups and have seen how it has been a real help for many.

We do not pretend to have covered the whole question of

life's beginnings, much less every aspect of sex education. And we realize that we have treated the issue in a manner which may seem random and incomplete. Moreover, since a child should have received a basic sex education by the time he or she is twelve or thirteen, we have limited our discussion to children of this age or younger. We have not attempted to deal with problems that might arise in later years.

In preparing this book, we interviewed about one hundred parents who had all made the effort to explain clearly and truthfully to their own children how life begins. All of them were Christian.

From our interviews we observed that parents themselves are not always completely free of certain inhibitions stemming from the education they received. The fact is that the present generation of parents, with the possible exception of the very youngest, has to a great extent had an inadequate education consisting mostly of silence, evasion, and denial. In spite of their earnest desires and good intentions, they have been conditioned in their approach to this topic. One young man, speaking for his wife and himself, told us, "We have had to make great efforts to free ourselves from the effects of the misguided education that was imparted to us."

On the other hand, good intentions and the desire to eliminate all difficulties in this area can themselves cause problems. For instance, timid parents, in the effort to overcome their own temperament, may get involved in lengthy explanations or assume such lively or exaggerated attitudes, that they call attention to themselves, the very thing they fear most. Other parents, in discussing with their children the topic of birth and human sexuality, fall into a superficial naturalism and optimism according to which everything is good, there are no dangers from which children should be protected, and no instincts which should be controlled. Such an attitude does not take into account the actual condition of weak human nature. In their efforts to be free and open about sex, these people insist upon considering it as no different from any other issue.

The ideal solution to the question lies, as always, in a

proper balance. It is necessary for parents to be relaxed and free in regard to the topic of sex, it is true, but they must also be aware of the formative influence they are to have upon their children.

The most positive element that we encountered in our experiences with parents was their sincere effort to conquer their fears and search for the right path to follow. Further, it was interesting to discover how their discussions with their children were educational (and perhaps even therapeutic) for themselves as well.

"I became aware," one parent commented, "how much our manner of facing and answering our childrens' questions reveals about our own ease or tension in this area. Many times in fact, moments such as these provide an occasion for us to investigate our own feelings and to clarify our own positions." This sentiment was echoed several times by the people we interviewed.

At the end of our interview with Mary N. she told us: "I feel that my own sex education was completed when my son, eleven years old, finally asked me the ultimate question about fertilization. As I sought to treat his question with love and to present things with some sense of their mystery and beauty, I finally felt myself freed from the last trace of the complexes that had been an obstacle to me in this area. Now I feel I could speak calmly with any child, even if he were not my own, and help him discover the golden thread of Divine Providence that runs through all creation."

Although we quote only about twenty of the persons we interviewed, we have tried to present the variety of their viewpoints, temperaments, backgrounds, family situations and so forth.

We would have liked to include more personal data about them, but the delicacy of some of the replies dissuaded us from doing so.

M.Q.

The explanation of the origin of
life to one's children is not just a
matter of imparting information but
involves the whole process of sex
education.

Chapter 1
Children Have The Right To
Know How They Were Born

Education of the whole person

Explaining the origin of life to our children is not just a matter of providing information but involves the more general field of sex education, which, in turn, is part of the whole educative process.

"I feel," confided one mother, "that this type of education involves much more than imparting specific information. I try to take advantage of every occasion, to be attentive to each moment, to act with delicacy and caution as well as timeliness."

Arthur M., a doctor, informed us of the main points in his discussion with his children about the origin of human life and matters of sex and continued: "The fact remains that this is not the end of the matter. It is only information. The most difficult part remains ahead, that of giving our children a true education, so that while respecting their freedom and without passing judgment on anyone who has a divergent opinion, we can instill genuine moral values and lead them to appropriate patterns of behavior."

Alice M. affirmed during our conversations: "In discussing this subject with our children, we must not neglect to consider the fact that human beings need to be formed in a complete way; we must endeavor to deal with the whole person, who is both body and spirit. Not only that, but this work of educating is constant and ongoing. There is not one hour during the day in which we educate our children and another in which we do not. I feel that education occurs during all twenty-four hours, even when we are alone. In other words, it goes on all life long. Now life involves relationship, relationship with God and with our neighbor. And that is what we are dealing with here."

"We must realize," as Stephen L. reminded us, "that sexuality is a complex matter that goes far beyond the physical relationship between a man and a woman. All humanity is sexual, but in a way which is much more profound than we normally think. Woman is complementary to man not only in physical structure, but in psychological, intellectual, and emotional makeup as well. In fact, even those who do not marry must seek wholeness and be open to the opposite sex. Those who remain celibate, for example, never reach maturity unless they find in God and in social relationships this completeness which others normally find in marriage. We say *normally* because very often the coalescence of all male and female elements does not occur even in marriage. In many couples love never reaches maturity (that is, it does not embrace all areas); many times, in fact, it does not get beyond the physical level. This is why so many marriages fail. Only when a man and woman complement one another in every aspect and give themselves to one another in every sense do they have a true bond of love."

Grace B. related: "When my friend Mary became engaged, she told me that the thought of marital relations gave her some anxiety. Then I explained that they are totally natural to a relationship. We can speak of physical unity, yes, but spiritual unity is first required as a foundation. When this is present the other comes spontaneously."

The necessary atmosphere

We have spoken of a complete education. Our children receive this not so much by listening to talks as by living in an "atmosphere" which is in itself formative and by being able to look to their parents as models and guides. This brings us to a theory recurrent in modern education, that it is the whole environment which educates us and not so much an individual teacher.

Here are some ideas selected from our interviews:

"Children put sexuality in proper perspective when they see it lived. We must open the door of life to them fully, speaking also of the marriage relationship. For when they see their father and mother living a normal life, they will see sexual relations in the proper perspective, as something normal, profound and beautiful, but above all normal, not something morbid or strange. What enlightens them more than words is the language of the soul, the life of the soul." (Alice M.)

"Before talking with the children, I tried to live this aspect of my life well, nurturing within me a profound love for my husband and great respect for the children." (Esther G.)

"To tell the truth, my husband and I confronted the problem of sex education and the beginning of life by trying to live every day with profound respect for life itself. Our children grew up in this atmosphere, with a sense of wonder for the life that is unfolding." (Grace B.)

For this atmosphere itself to be formative, and for

children to see themselves reflected in their parents, husband and wife must truly love each other and must cultivate between them this complete communion which we have mentioned. This is a well-known principle of child psychology.

But the question always arises: is it good for children to see their parents showing affection for one another?

The interviews revealed various types of behavior which did not however indicate differing opinions. Here are two examples:

Alice M. states: "David and I are not the type to display our feelings or our love for one another before our children. Perhaps we are somewhat reserved in our behavior."

Esther G. offers: "Anthony and I find little difficulty in sharing our feelings in front of our children, a kiss, for example, a caress, some manifestation of affection, but done without great display. I have always stressed to them the importance of love in marriage and it seems to me that these small incidents confirm what I try to say."

Here we want to point out, as our interviews confirmed, that it does not really matter whether there are outward manifestations of love or not. Each person should do what his temperament dictates, and be spontaneous. What really matters is the presence of love, love that is beautiful, profound, complete, generous and constantly growing; this is what children notice from a very early age. This is the atmosphere that molds them, strengthens them spiritually and carries them through negative experiences.

It is this atmosphere that reveals the true origin of

life: love. If father and mother are always trying to make their love grow and reach full maturity, if children see their parents continuously reaching out to one another and to the children as well, discussions concerning birth and fertilization will take place in a simple and warm way and seem like a logical consequence of love.

When that kind of relationship exists between parents and children, sex education will have a proper foundation. In fact, the secret of sex education is in this fundamental principle: nothing must be done out of selfishness, or the desire to possess, or for one's own pleasure or reward.

If parents by their lives as well as their words, educate their children in love and convince them that true satisfaction is found only in the gift of self, then behavioral deviations and sexual vices will not present any real threat.

When children receive this kind of education, there is some guarantee that they will eventually marry not in order to have someone to lean on or to take advantage of, but in order to have someone to sustain and to love sincerely.

This leads us to a further conclusion. Sexuality is an energy, a dynamic force, a drive toward self-fulfillment which everyone feels. When this force is directed toward love, even people who have dedicated their lives to virginity may find fulfillment in dedicating themselves to others. Since sexuality reaches maturity when it becomes a gift of oneself to another, then a celibate who loves everyone he or she meets obviously does not remain incomplete and unfulfilled but instead enriches all humanity.

The task belongs to the parents

We can never place enough stress on the importance of children asking their first questions of their
parents and getting their first replies directly from
them. Every aspect of this subject, which deals ulti-
mately with love, requires for its proper treatment the
natural setting of the family, the miniature society
which is supposed to be founded on love.

In fact children, who live more by intuition than by
reasoning, naturally feel the need to ask their parents
these questions, if they have the opportunity. Many
times, a child who has been told something by someone
outside the family will come to his parents for further
explanation, and when he finds that their responses
satisfy his needs, he will decide on his own not to confide any more in outsiders. For example, Francis C.,
after an exhaustive explanation by his mother, exclaimed, "You know, I'm not going to listen to what my
friends say anymore. I'll come ask you everything."

Then there was Anita P., nine years old, who
helped a friend who wanted some information on this
topic. Her mother told us: "One time at a meeting with
several families, we were taking a break and one mother
went out into the garden to nurse her newborn baby.
Some children happened to be playing nearby. One little
girl stopped to watch and was very impressed by what
she saw, probably because she had never had the opportunity to see a mother nurse her baby. She came over to
ask an explanation from Anita who replied, 'A baby
comes from his mother, and God has planned it that
while he is small she can feed him by holding him close.
But if you want to find out about this, ask your mother

and father because they can explain it best. You will see how wonderful it all is when they explain it to you.'

"The next day, the mother of Anita's friend thanked me because Anita's statement was the beginning of their discussion on this subject."

Her little brother, after listening to his parents describe how a birth takes place, exclaimed, "How nice it is to talk about these things with you! When I talk with other children, it's not the same. Things just aren't as beautiful as when you talk about them."

It is the parents who have the task of informing and educating their children in these matters; they also are the ones who best know their own children and how to treat them. Therefore it is wise to tell children, when they have received this information, not to pass it on to friends and classmates.

"Each time I speak with my girls," Monica M. told us, "I remind them not to say anything to other children. I add that this is something beautiful and it is to be kept in the family. Every mother and father want to tell these things personally to their own children."

Marcia P. related, "Our twin girls who are still attending nursery school are already aware of many of these things. I was afraid that they might shock other children by informing them about things for which they might not be prepared. I advised them not to discuss this subject with their girl friends because their fathers and mothers are the ones who should do this."

At times such caution is necessary to avoid annoying other parents, who might not yet have explained the truth to their children.

It seems that Caroline C. made a wise decision. She said, "When Fred was in first grade, one day he came home and said to me, 'You know, mom, a friend of mine told me that a baby sister arrived at his house, and just think, his mother told him that a stork brought her.' " He was dumbfounded.

" 'It was probably because your friend likes fairy tales,' I explained. 'Therefore his mother thought she would tell it like a tale. Do you know why? Every mother knows her own child best and knows what to tell him. For this reason it is best to go to your mother and ask her to explain it. This is better than discussing it with other children.' "

Relationship of confidence and trust

If it is in the family that children should find the proper "climate" for a well-balanced formation and if it is from their parents that they should get the facts, then there must be an open and relaxed atmosphere which will permit children to converse freely and to ask personal questions of their parents rather than of outsiders.

"From the time our children were very young," related Arthur M., "my wife and I have always tried to encourage their confidence in us. Later when they became older and began to go to school, I said to them openly, 'Any time you have questions on any subject, ask us.' " Even the question of sexuality and how life begins came up and was discussed. Not that we feel that we have completely resolved all our children's problems about sex. Naturally, our children will have problems, as everyone will, but we hope we have helped them a little by removing the aura of mystery and above all by having initiated a 'dialogue,' as people say these days. If they do have problems we hope they will have the confidence to talk with us, as in fact they have done so far, instead of consulting other people."

Gloria I., mother and doctor said, "It is important for children to be able to ask their questions without embarrassment."

This statement also reaffirms a fundamental peda-gogical principle: there can be no education unless a kind of exchange is established between the educator and the learner. Now, if our child were to come to ask us how babies are born or whether it is possible to have children without being married, we should be thrilled. The most important thing is that our children have confidence and trust in us.

"I will begin immediately by saying," explained Caroline C. as soon as we began our interview, "that I suffered greatly as a child because in my family there was a lot of love but not much trust. I found it very difficult to confide in my mother and this is something very important for a young girl. I reached the age of puberty and began growing up with many questions still on my mind, and I did not know whom to ask. Then, unfortunately, I found a girl who was worldly wise. She explained these things to me the wrong way, which created a lot of anxiety in me. As a result I have been deeply concerned that my children not go through such an experience. Therefore when I married I wanted to be sure to instill in my children this sense of trust that my own parents had failed to give to me.

"Now that my children are grown, I realize that this rapport does exist. I achieved it by always speaking the truth, even if many times, because of my own inner anxieties, I was embarrassed and came close to ruining everything."

Relationship of truth and love

From this experience comes another fundamental idea: the best way to create a trustful relationship with children is to tell them the truth at all times, even when they are very young.

A sound relationship of love cannot be based on anything but truth. Deception is always due to a lack of love. We can say that this has been the central issue in all the interviews.

Among other things, Grace B. told us, "The thing that seems so important to me is to gain the respect of the other person, whatever the situation may be. When the other person is a child, he or she is innocent, unknowing and above all inexperienced, and must be treated with respect. Therefore, be sure to respond in a way worthy of a child of God. We cannot deceive them with the excuse that they will not understand; that would clearly be contrary to the will of God."

This was confirmed by Martha S. as she explained her past mistake: "Just as I was to enter the hospital, Lucy asked me how the baby would come out. Here I made an unpardonable error. My daughter seemed too young to understand the truth. In reality, it was I who, without realizing it, had a mental block on this point. And so I said that in the hospital I would be cut open, something which turned out to be more traumatic for her than I could ever have imagined, as I discovered later.

"After the birth of the baby, Lucy came to visit me in the hospital, to see me and the little brother who had been so anxiously awaited. But her only concern was for me. She caressed me with a great tenderness because she saw me in bed and knew that I had suffered in order to give life to her little brother. Then she asked me to show her the cut in my stomach. If it had been true I would gladly have shown it to her, but there was nothing to show. She took up the question again, 'But mommy, do you have to be cut open for every baby?' It was obvious that the problem bothered her and that she was still worried about it. At this moment I began to realize what a mistake I had made. When you decide, as I finally did, to tell the truth, it is necessary to be consistent. It is far better to postpone a talk until the child is more mature than to deliberately mislead. Even if you believe that when they ask an explicit question they are able to understand the answer, you must adapt your reply to their age. And the best way to reply is to explain how God made things. So I backed up a bit and told her the truth. Lucy watched me with eyes full of untold reverence. I realized that she understood everything I said, and that our relationship was beginning to deepen."

The more children are treated with respect and told the truth, the more they trust their parents and open up more easily. They begin to 'communicate,' as we say. Then the more free, relaxed and spontaneous they are in asking their questions, the easier it is to create a "climate" favorable to their complete formation and to tell them the whole truth.

"I would like to say," Marcia P. offered, "that taking the time to speak with our children on this subject has not been, as we might imagine, either embarrassing or difficult. We would say instead that we have had moments of discussion which were very beautiful for everyone, isn't it true, Brian?" she asked her husband, who confirmed her statement.

Esther G. said, "Every time that the girls confided their doubts to us or asked us questions, we responded to their needs and felt a strengthening of unity and love among us, which left in them a profound sense of joy and closeness. Today, for example, when I left to come here, I told them that I would return soon and that later we would be together for awhile to talk about some small decisions; one of them said to me, 'Mommy, will it be nice like the other day when you explained all those things to us?' In reply to their questions, I had described fertilization and had spent almost all morning with them completely forgetting about all the things I was supposed to be doing."

One aspect of "telling the truth" is to use the correct names for the genital organs. And if we don't know the exact terminology, we should find out.

Arthur M., a doctor, said, "We have always called the various organs by their true names without a fuss. A nose is a nose, and a penis is a penis."

Alice M. said, "When I told George that the uterus contains and protects the little fetus, I spoke of a 'tiny room.' This was the only time, however, that I used other than specific language. I feel it is always better to use words that are true, even if substitute images may be more meaningful for some children."

Above all, giving children the possibility to refer to the genital organs by their precise names diminishes their desire to use so-called "dirty words" among themselves.

The importance of the father's presence

In our desire to gather parents' experiences in explaining the facts of life to their children, at first we instinctively approached mothers. When we asked ourselves why we had made this unconscious choice, we realized that it was much easier to enter a discussion of this type with mothers. Why? One very plausible reason is that fathers, because of their traditional role as wage-earners, have much less contact with their children than do mothers. While this may be true, it is not the only reason. Another reason, and one which is more discouraging, is that generally fathers become involved with the educative process of their children either too little or too late. Many have limited rapport with their children, shrugging off their own responsibility and passing it on to their wives. However, this was not the case with the families whom we approached, who for the most part live in harmony, with good will toward one another, and with husbands anything but unconcerned about the problem. We are dealing here with a very practical matter. At an early age children have quite an interest in the matter of birth and everything connected with it. However, even if the father is present when they raise their first questions, it is usually the mother who initially speaks about maternity, because she feels directly called to answer.

Later, except perhaps in cases where the father is a doctor or where he has a particularly warm relationship with his children, the dialogue which originated with the mother will tend to continue with her even in instances where the topic would relate more directly to the father.

Here we would like to stress that this does not necessarily imply that children relate only with the mother, even when that seems to be the case and the father remains excluded.

If the position of the father remains indistinct in the family relationship, grave harm may result. Although children can identify with the parent of either sex, boys who have difficulty identifying with their fathers may find it hard to arrive at maturity and may even risk becoming homosexual.

"Yes, it is true," admitted Mary N. "Luke approached me with his first questions and continued to do so when his father was absent. But each time I related everything to my husband and I can truly say that he participated actively in the formation of our son. If I had not had a profound understanding with him and his full support, it is possible that I could have ruined everything. I do not really believe that Luke asked his questions purposely at the moment when his father was absent."

So, even if children turn more frequently to their mother, this need not exclude the father, since discussions of this sort arise quite spontaneously when the entire family is together, as at dinner or in the car, for example.

Esther G. said, "It shows how much freedom our daughters feel to ask questions in the presence of Anthony, my husband, that even though they are girls, they ask the most serious and challenging ones when we are eating, and without the least hesitation."

Brian P., an artist, offered: "Our children almost always presented their questions to Marcia, but usually I was there too and entered into the discussion."

After his wife had described the circumstances in which their eldest daughter asked her first question, Timothy P., a contractor, added, "To me it is important that I was able to be present at the beginning, because we were able to discuss these things together. In this way a greater rapport developed as we worked at it together."

The presence of the paternal figure, at least in spirit, is very important here, as in every other sector of education. We would say it is especially important here for creating an atmosphere where the husband and wife can introduce the children to the man-woman relationship in its beautiful natural setting.

Isabel C. is one of our friends who was widowed at a very early age, with one child three years old and another eighteen months. She said, "When Neil died, in addition to the almost unbearable pain of losing him, I was terrified by the idea of raising and educating our girls by myself. Neil had such clear ideas on this subject and was naturally disposed to take an active role in the education of our children. I did not feel that I had the ability to carry out the task that he would have done so well. Later, however, when I began to get my thoughts in order, I meditated a lot on the communion of saints and the relationship between those in heaven and those on earth and I understood that I would still be able to count on my husband's assistance. Every time I received Jesus in the Eucharist, I felt closer to Neil too and I confided in him and entrusted my problems to him. The scriptures also helped me. To tell the truth, it turned out to be a beautiful experience. It seems that my daughters are developing without anxiety. The figure of their father is so strongly present that the girls do not seem to be suffering from the shock of losing him."

Many times, however, mothers or fathers, in spite of their concern to give their children a good sound education, cannot depend on the collaboration of their spouses. Is their action then destined to failure?

We can learn from the reply of Susan S., the coura-

geous mother of three boys: "We should not forget that
if we raise our children with faith in God who is Love
and who is our Father, the most important fatherly
relationship will never be lacking in their lives. From
the moment my husband left me in order to remarry, I
have always tried not to lose sight of this reality. When I
am in difficulty, or when the children ask me something
and I don't know exactly what line to follow, I turn to
God and say to him with great simplicity, 'Look, you
have entrusted these boys to me, but they are your children. Help me, otherwise I may ruin them for you.' In
every instance I have been guided to the proper action
and peace has returned to my soul. The children are
really well-adjusted, and I can say this without pride for
it is not my doing. They always confide in me about
their friends and teachers. For me this is an important
verification."

A typical and interesting experience concerning
the paternal role in the dialogue was related to us by
Marianne and George M., adoptive parents of two
delightful little girls.

"Perhaps because neither of us has physically given
life to these girls, we both entrust them to God. In our
family there is not even that natural distinction of roles
for father and mother that normally exists in other
families.

"With respect to questions about conception, birth
and sexuality, it is the same to our girls whether they
ask Marianne or myself. Often it depends merely on
who is nearby. When we are both present, sometimes
they ask me and sometimes they ask Marianne.

"It is very important to us since our children are
adopted that they approach us in this way, because this

helps create an atmosphere of true community and real trust within the family."

There is no best time or place for beginning the discussion: it should be spontaneous

The first thing that parents ask themselves is: "When is the proper time to go beyond just creating an educational atmosphere and start presenting the facts of life?

"At what age," they ask, "should we start talking about it?"

The answer was clearly provided during the course of our interviews.

"In my experience as mother of five children, two girls and three boys," said Alice M., "I have seen that it is not a matter of age; each child has its own timing. There are many factors; it depends primarily on the general maturity of the child—including his spiritual maturity—when sexuality assumes an important place in his social and emotional life and in his general development."

Everyone's experience suggests: There is no particular age at which to begin, because children mature in different ways. This is something to keep in mind; the discussion should take place spontaneously and naturally.

We cannot realistically expect to sit down with our children on an appointed day and say to them, "Now I want to explain to you how babies are born." Yet many parents actually do proceed in this manner. However, since questions, answers and circumstances arise naturally, they cannot be foreseen and rehearsed as a teacher, psychologist or family doctor might do. (We need not hesitate to use such professional assistance when helpful.)

If children are not too timid to speak and above all if they feel comfortable with their parents, then when the right moment arises they will simply pose their first question. This is the time to begin! The conversation must be simple and informal, not like a lesson or a sermon, as is so often the case when parents take a professional approach or when they are embarrassed by "such a delicate topic."

Children generally respond with open ears because they simply want information. They have no inhibitions and will not develop them, provided we do not give them ours because of our mistaken attitudes.

For children this is a topic like any other, to be discussed naturally. But they do have a way of posing their first questions at the least opportune time and place, as far as we are concerned. Often, for example, younger brothers and sisters are present when we would like to talk to a child privately at the moment that seems best for him. To judge from our experience, questions usually seem to come up at the dinner table.

Generally, when we are gathered together for a meal, we all relax a little. The children sense the casual intimacy and discussion can develop freely. Suddenly comes a new insight. When a problem arises in their minds, they simply ask a question, and since we are right there we can at once resolve the problem and ease the tension. But we must be there to assist them.

Marcia P. laughingly described how her child's first questions were brought up precisely at dinner time:

"It had been a long day of hard work. You know how it is when you flop down at the dinner table, exhausted? Larry, seven years old, like a bolt out of the blue, asked, 'Mommy how are babies born?' At first I felt totally overwhelmed, especially after a day like the one I had been through. A question like that at dinner time and with the five-year-old twins right there was just too much! I really drew a blank. But only for a moment. Then I began with an explanation that was the most simple and direct: 'Babies are formed inside their mother...' It did not matter that the younger children were also present. There would be another time when I could have a personal talk with each one."

Here is what Andrew, a doctor, said: "My wife and I had discussed the problem of how to bring up the discussion with our children, but in a very general way. That is, we had simply agreed to tell them the truth. Beyond that, we would be guided by the circumstances. Above all, we planned to be as ready to reply to any questions on the subject of sex as on any other topic, to avoid any secretive atmosphere. If there is good rapport, a child will ask his parents all kinds of questions. There is the age of 'why' and we always try to give some answer. Many times the children ask their questions at the dinner table and we answer them at the dinner table. There is the older one, the younger one, and the toddler. That does not matter. Each one takes in what interests him. I have noticed that if the conversation is not interesting to one of them, he simply doesn't bother to listen."

Many others said the same thing. For example, Esther G. said, "The first three children, who are very close in age, have always participated in these discus-

sions together. The discussions often occur at the table
and it is most often Chris, the eldest, who asks the
questions. For this reason, I never have the heart to say,
"I'll explain it to you, but not to them,' and send the
other two away. If I did, they would have felt excluded
from the family circle. Instead I gave an explanation
that was directed to all of them. But I could see that
comprehension varied from child to child."

"Naturally then," observed Paul R., after he had
said the same thing, "if necessary we pursue the conversation at some other time with the child who first raised
the question, and we look for a time when we can be
alone with him without making it obvious."

"In fact," affirmed Alice M., "when a family is large
it is difficult to find a time to be alone with one child.
But I have noticed that, when it is necessary, an opportunity will present itself. For example, it was some time
before I was able to continue this discussion on a deeper
level with Mark. But I waited because it was necessary to
be calm and find a time when we would not be interrupted. Finally, last summer, when we were on vacation
at our cottage, some relatives came to visit for a week-
end, so I had to share Mark's room with him and the
conversation developed spontaneously."

But let us get back to what we were saying: one
time and place is as good as another.

Alice continued: "One day I was in church at Mass
with George. I saw him absorbed and assumed that he
was deep in prayer. Then all at once he looked at me.
'Mommy, I can't remember any more how babies are
born,' and right then and there he wanted all the
details."

Martha S. said, "We were all together in the car,

returning from our vacation. We were talking about something else. Suddenly, Lucy, who was sitting in back, interrupted us and asked, 'How can a mother know when a baby is coming?'"

"Another time that children like to choose," observed Mary N., "is at night when they are preparing for bed. We like to leave them relaxed and peaceful, so we try to end the day with a few tender moments. During the day they have not had time because they are too busy playing, but while they are putting on their pajamas they freely express their thoughts and their reflections. If nothing else, they instinctively think of pretexts for postponing the moment when they have to crawl under the covers, because having to go to sleep while their parents are still up gives them the feeling of being excluded from the family circle. No excuse works better than an urgent question.

"I don't know why, but as soon as I say to Luke, 'It's time to go to sleep, good night!' the most pressing theological, scientific, moral and psychological questions immediately arise."

Questions develop gradually and should not be put off

Many times parents are uneasy about the thought of telling their children about the facts of life, because they fear that they must immediately deal with sexual relations. They are especially afraid of destroying their image in the eyes of their children or presenting the subject in a bad light.

In fact, however, children never ask all their questions at once. Their interests and their needs develop gradually and so they raise their questions gradually. Between one question and another there is always an interlude, sometimes a long one of several months or years while the child assimilates the information he has received. Very often the same question is asked again later on because the child has matured and wants to deepen his knowledge.

At first children want to know how they were born. "Where do babies come from?" Their interest in the connection between the formation of the baby in the mother and the role of the father comes much later.

"I remember," Mary N. told us, "that from the very beginning I spoke of the male seed fertilizing the female seed, but only later did I see that this talk of seed was incomprehensible to Luke. Only when he was eleven did he ask about fertilization, and then he listened to my explanation as if it were the first time I had spoken of it."

Questions develop gradually and we can calmly accompany our children step by step without undue concern if we free ourselves from our own guilt and fears. The various stages along the way will become clear and through the love we have for our children we will find the light to respond in an adequate way. To avoid creating anxiety, misconceptions, and wrong attitudes, we must be careful that our own apprehension or unpreparedness does not cause us to evade the question or postpone answering. The child is awaiting the solution to his problem, and if we do not provide it he will turn to someone else.

"It is never pedagogically useful to put off the answer," affirmed Andrew M., the doctor. "This is particularly true in sex education. If a child senses his parents avoiding the subject, it will have negative implications for him."

Of course, at times it will be useful or even necessary (as when children ask at the most inappropriate times) to wait for an opportune moment when the topic can be pursued in a more favorable atmosphere.

"When babies are so big how can they get out?" asked Monica's six-year-old adoptive daughter one day at the table. Because Monica and her husband had guests for dinner, "we were forced to do something which ordinarily we never do: postpone our talk till another time, because we realized that this matter required a more calm and intimate setting."

However, such a delay should be kept as brief as possible.

Paul R. comments: "If one of our boys needs a more complete answer to a question which he asked before the entire family, I might say, 'When you have a little time we'll talk about it some more.' Then I do all I can to remember to continue the conversation with him soon again, because the worst we can do is to disappoint the children after we have promised them a reply."

Reasons for not giving an immediate response can vary considerably. There is no fixed rule. Every mother and father can sense when it is not the right time. Sometimes, for example, we may delay the conversation until bedtime because we know that the atmosphere at that time will be more peaceful and we can take advantage of that moment of quiet at the end of the day.

As Annmarie P. described: "When Ann returned from school and asked me to explain how a baby is born, the younger children were playing nearby and creating a lot of confusion by running in and out of the room. If I had tried to sit and talk with Ann, the others would not have been quiet. On the other hand, I did not want to disappoint her, so I said that after supper, when the younger children were in bed and everything was quiet, we would be able to talk. In fact, after supper my husband and I both sat down to talk with her."

But in other circumstances, when a child is unsettled or unable to get to sleep or when his question is more complicated, parents may decide that bedtime is not the right time. They may fear acting unwisely and spoiling the talk. "It was precisely the question about fertilization," Esther G. said, "that came up one evening. I said to the children, 'Look, it is late now, and there is not really enough time to talk about all of this. Let's do it tomorrow.' I purposely postponed it because if the girls had become disturbed they would not have slept. The next day, however, when they were at home because school had not yet begun, I spent the morning discussing the subject with them."

Wait for the question

On the other hand we can run into the opposite danger. If we are overly concerned not to avoid the question or delay our answer or if we are too eager to get rid of our "taboos" and not be taken by surprise, we may try to offer a complete dissertation on the process of fertilization as soon as the first question is asked. Therefore, it is most important to ascertain how much the child really wants to know from the way the question is asked, so we can limit ourselves to that alone.

Several parents have reiterated this point.

Here is what Andrea M. had to say: "If a question

arises in our girls' minds, we endeavor to reply with the truth, to be precise and to the point, without going beyond the particular question."

Andrew M. remarked, "From the beginning my wife and I were prepared to answer the children's questions as they were presented but we limited ourselves to the question itself."

Marcia P. related, "When Larry asked me how babies are born, I replied that they are formed inside their mother. Mothers are made in a special way to allow the baby to grow inside them.' And I stopped there. I answered his question and no more, without going on to awaken other needs that perhaps had not matured in him. At that moment in fact Larry was satisfied. After a month his next question arrived on schedule. 'But if they are born from the mother, then they must grow inside the mother.' He did not bother to give the sentence a subject; he seemed to be continuing a discussion interrupted only a few minutes before. 'And how do they eat?' This question I also answered in a simple and succinct way, adding nothing more. And this is what happened each time."

One thing that surprised many parents was that when they prolonged the discussion too much, the children were already fully satisfied and interrupted them by going on to some other topic.

"Each time I gave a fancy explanation that extended beyond the interest of the moment, Luke would immediately say, 'I understand, thanks mom!' And he would leave me in the middle of a sentence," confessed Mary N.

Tom P. said, "The child himself is saying, 'That's enough. Don't tell me any more!' He understands that these are things which must be discovered gradually, in due time."

Andrew M. offered: "While our girls were washing and preparing for bed, Ann started up the discussion which had been interrupted at the table: 'Then, daddy,' she said, 'how can such big babies come out of the mother?' I began to explain to her that when babies are born they are very small, and also that the providence of God plans everything so that they can come out easily, with the help of the doctor. However, while I was still trying to tell her how marvelous it was, how it all happened so naturally and how the inside of the mother could expand, Ann, who was satisfied with the first part of the answer and saw that the rest was too complicated for her, finished washing and simply walked away without listening to another word."

There are no set answers and no typical children

When parents have decided that they want to speak nothing but the truth to their children, they should prepare themselves with a precise outline they can follow. Advance preparation is necessarily limited. Parents can obtain basic anatomical, physiological and psychological facts, and plan in a general way how to orient the discussion, how to act and what to say. But it is impossible to offer parents a fully prepared talk, complete with periods, commas, phrasing, with examples and illustrations, all correlated with sketches, designs and photographs.

There are many reasons and they are fairly evident. The fundamental reason is this: each person is an individual with a distinct personality; each situation is unique.

It is quite impossible to write a talk that is equally satisfactory for parents who are blue collar workers, doctors, scientists, teachers, philosophers, artists, widows, talented or uneducated. Each person must prepare his own explanation, on the basis of his own background, his own awareness and his own natural attributes.

For similar reasons it is not possible to prepare a standard discourse for a typical child. Children are very different from one another, even those in the same family, coming from the same social and cultural environment. Some children are more precise than others, some more specific, some more aesthetic. There are those for whom the problem of sex is especially difficult, those who lean to fantasy, stories, or poetry; there are those more introverted, more reserved, more reticent, some who do not even have the courage to ask questions; others are more open, more sociable, or perhaps more easily distracted.

One child might ask a specific question at an early age and another the very same question at a much later age. One child may be a member of a large family, and another an only child.

Each child requires a different way of presenting things. This is a very positive feature because the dialogue will be fresh each time. Even if a mother and father speak five separate times with their five children, they must create a fresh rapport with each one.

Caroline C. stated: "I had already explained many things to Frederick, who is the elder, when Tina, four years younger, began to ask her first questions. I thought it would be so much easier with Tina since I had already had some experience and felt better prepared and able to avoid mistakes. Instead it was not so easy. Frederick, perhaps because he is a boy, wanted everything precise and from a more or less scientific point of view. Tina, instead, is all fantasy. If I told her everything as it stands, without a full complement of details and stories, she would not be satisfied. For this reason I had to explain things to her in a different way, in a more sentimental and poetic manner, with illustrations and examples."

Anthony and Monica, adoptive parents, explained their situation to us, an unusual one which required a special approach.

"We should preface this by explaining that we adopted our first child even before she was born; therefore we had no idea what sex she would be. When we decided to adopt a second child so that she would not be alone, we chose another girl and planned to tell them they were adopted without making an issue about it. What we want to say, however, is this: that we are convinced that when it comes to dealing with sex, our children subconsciously resent the circumstances of their birth. As we see it, the fact that they were not wanted and accepted, that their parents did not have a true union, left a deep psychological mark on them.

"One of our children, the elder, displays a particular sensitivity about the problem, a certain cynicism, we might say, in dealing with it. So much so that we make a decided effort to present everything very openly in a positive light, as absolutely normal and without hidden foreboding. We try never to be shocked by their discussions, their questions, or their attitudes, but to deal with everything in a calm, simple and direct way."

The conclusion to all this is quite obvious. Fathers and mothers who truly love their children, who make the effort to put themselves on their level and to understand them, usually find an accurate and appropriate way of expressing themselves, even if they have no formal knowledge of education or psychology.

Evidently this demands great dedication on the part of the parents, who will often fear being inadequate for such an important task and afraid of taking false steps in such a delicate area.

"I remember, said Esther G., 'how my heart pounded when Chris, the eldest, asked her first, you might say, *official* question. At that moment, I prayed for guidance. And I told Chris very simply how, after the annunciation of the Angel, Mary carried Jesus inside her for nine months."

Grace B. said, "Certainly it is very difficult, but it is necessary to trust that Divine Providence is with us moment by moment, giving us the grace to answer our children in the right way according to the needs of each one. This should all be done in God's presence.

"We should pause for a brief prayer, 'God please give me a hand, help me.' And then we speak from our heart, whether the child is one year old or twenty. It's all the same because he is a child of God who is developing and facing new problems and difficulties."

Paula R. related this episode: "Alan, the second of our four children, never mentioned any personal problems, never asked any questions. He was always content with the family discussions we had at dinner or wherever, without asking anything further. All of a sudden, one day when he was in junior high school, he returned home and came right up to me. I was preparing dinner and Greg, my husband, and the other children had not yet arrived. We went to the window to watch for them. He leaned on the window sill and said to me, 'Mom, I have to ask you something. I don't really know... how does marriage happen or, rather, how does the sex act take place between husband and wife?' To tell the truth, facing this boy as old as he was, I really felt ill at ease, and it seemed more than I could handle. But, I said to myself, 'If he comes to me, I cannot tell him: ask your father. And I don't know if he would find the occasion to ask this question again.' It is so important to seize the opportunity and not back off. I realized that his asking me this question in such a simple and direct way was a most precious gift. Nevertheless, I felt the need to ask Mary for help. In one second I said silently, 'Mary, give me the right words to explain all this to him,' and I began to speak. I would never be able to repeat what I said to him; there arose such a closeness between us that everything came out easily and clearly. I know that I hid nothing and that our conversation was really blessed. So much that my son was neither shocked nor disappointed. This was my impression: he was satisfied not just humanly but also spiritually. These two areas were not in conflict; there was a harmony between them. It seemed to me that after our conversation Alan was more mature in every way."

It began like this

Parents who are open seize the first opportunity offered them to begin presenting the facts of life. It would be best to let several of the mothers we interviewed relate how their discussions began and how they presented their first explanations.

Mary S. said: "I began by explaining the words of Elizabeth to Mary: 'Blessed is the fruit of your womb.' Many other incidents followed this first discussion, like the time a pediatrician made a house call to see one of our children on Christmas Eve. Naturally the children wanted to show him the crib they were so proud of. He looked for the infant in the manger, but when he didn't find him, he teasingly said to the children, 'What kind of a crib is this? The baby Jesus isn't even here!' Chris, who was then four years old, looked at him with exasperation and said, 'But it isn't Christmas yet. He's still inside Mary.'"

Often, it is a new pregnancy that provides an occasion, many parents told us, or, at times, it may be the pregnancy of some relative or friend of the family. Martha S. said, "The occasion to tell my children the facts of life arose when I was expecting our third child, Peter. Lucy was three and a half and Sam, two and a half. Often I played with them, any game they liked, and sometimes we played ball. One time the ball went under the sofa, and I, by then in my fourth month, did not feel like crawling after it as I usually did. Lucy was annoyed. 'Mommy won't play with us anymore,' she said. At that moment it seemed wise for me to justify my behavior, so I took advantage of the occasion to talk to them. I sat down near Lucy and Sam listened in too, because he always stayed close to his sister.

"I told them that a new brother or sister would join the family in a while. Immediately they wanted to know more about it. Therefore I explained that mommy would soon grow fatter because a baby is growing inside her. For nine months she carries him inside her because he is so small and delicate that he does not know how to take care of himself. And mommy feeds him by letting him live inside her. When he is born he will have to be dressed and fed until he is able to do those things by himself, just like them. I noticed the children's faces light up; they were happy. During those nine months they watched me as I grew larger, because it meant the little baby was growing. In the evening when I put them to bed they wanted to say 'good night' to the baby, too. I remember when they first felt him move. They rested their heads on my stomach and jumped up radiant. Lucy exclaimed happily, 'He said hello to me.'"

Gloria I. said, "This educational task began for me when I was expecting our fourth child. I do not remember the exact details, but I know that I told the two older children that a new baby was coming. Ellen was four and Fran three. Both of them were going to nursery school. I remember one day the teacher showed me a drawing Ellen had done. It was a rough sketch of the cradle where we would place the new baby. Already this event was in her thoughts.

"On one of the last days before the birth, I was fixing up the cradle, which was lined with material, and while I turned away for a moment, Ellen took a red pencil and scribbled on the fabric. She explained, 'I wrote Baby I.' (last name). This seemed like a way of saying that the baby was already a member of the family."

Grace B., who has seven children, stated, "One

time, when I was expecting a new child, I told the others, 'Do you know? In a little while we will have a new baby!' Together we decided where he would sleep, what we would prepare for him, and so on. Then I told them that the baby grows inside the mother for nine months. In that way they understood that their little sister or brother was already alive. And I let them know what a great joy this birth would be for our whole family."

Allowing the children to participate so intimately in the arrival of a new family member is such a wholesome thing. They know that the baby is already alive and they wait for him, although they do not suffer or get involved in the labor process. So by the time he is born the older children have learned to love the baby little by little, and his 'invasion' of the household is not so likely to be traumatic or lead to jealous rivalry.

At times the initial question is provoked by something outside the family. Children absorb everything: it is enough for them to hear one unfamiliar word and they immediately come and ask for an explanation.

When they go to school their companions may begin to tell them about all they know (or do not know), and it is up to us then, when they return home to straighten things out and put everything in proper light and balance.

"With Louise," Paula R. related, "it was like this. She had never seen anyone pregnant among our relatives and friends. Not even on the street did she ever seem to notice a woman being out of proportion. As a result she never raised any questions. Only later on did she begin to hear terms that she did not understand. It was then that she came to me and asked, 'What does pregnant mean?' or, 'What is delivery?' So we began there. By that time I was expecting Andrew, so I was able to explain a lot to her."

"One day," Annemarie P. told us, "Ann, the elder child, who at that time was about five years old, returned home from visiting a school friend. She confronted me with, 'Today Mary told me all about the stork. She said babies are really born from their mothers. She wanted me to promise not to tell you, so I wouldn't be punished. But I'm telling you because I want to know if she was telling the truth. If it is the truth you won't punish me, will you mommy?' 'That's right,' I replied. 'Come here and I will explain it all. It is something very beautiful. Listen....' While I was speaking, I saw how important it was for me to explain what her friend had presented so inadequately as happens so often."

Here is what Mary N. had to say: "It was summer time and we were on vacation at our cabin in the mountains. We had invited a young woman to spend a few days with us. She had been married for two years but had no children. It was a great disappointment for her. The presence of my little boy, happy, full of life and playful, served to emphasize her problem. One evening while we were praying and asking God to give his blessings and graces to all, she raised her voice and asked Luke, 'Why don't you ask Jesus to send me a little boy like you? I'm sure that if you ask, Jesus will listen!' Luke was happy and proud that such a great responsibility was entrusted to him. As tired as he was, he still wanted to offer a prayer that evening and he asked my assistance. The following morning, as soon as he was awake, still in his pajamas and before he even said 'good morning' to me, he ran into our guest's room. I heard him ask her, without a word of introduction, 'Well, did Jesus send you the baby?' As soon as I could I directed him to go out on the patio for breakfast. While he was eating I told him the beautiful story about the way babies come and how long it takes. 'Right inside their mommy?' 'Yes.' 'Can you hear his heart beat?' 'Yes.' Then, a little perplexed, he asked, 'Nine months, isn't that a long time?' 'Yes, it is.' 'As much time as it takes for Christmas to come?' 'More, almost twice as much.' 'How come so long?' I reminded him of a television documentary he had seen a short time before that showed in time-lapse photography the germination and development of a flower. I reminded him, 'Do you remember how the flower drinks water and draws from the earth and peeks out little by little? It grows, puts out leaves, then blossoms and opens up?' 'Yes, it was beautiful.' 'Well, a baby is really like a little seed, then slowly, slowly, safe and protected inside of his mother, he grows and takes shape until he is ready to be born.' 'I like that,' he said enthusiastically

"I was waiting for him to ask me more questions, but instead he took off his bib, picked up a pail and shovel and went off to play. He seemed very content and I thought it ended very well."

There are also cases when it seems that the opportune moment will never come. The child sees his mother pregnant, hears his parents speaking about birth, but never asks the question that will give them the chance to get the discussion going. Fairly often we heard mothers say, "My son is ten years old and he has never asked me a thing." Or: "My daughter will soon be maturing and she has never asked a single question. I don't know what to do."

There are many instances like that. If we find ourselves in this kind of situation, the first thing to do is to examine our conscience and ask ourselves: "Have I been able to establish with my child a relationship that will let him readily ask me any question, even on this topic?" "Have I lost too much time through cowardice so that my child is now too old for me to treat this problem naturally and easily?" If so, we must hurry to correct the situation and try to gain the child's trust and confidence. Then we should try to find out how much he knows and what his problems may be, since our false attitudes may have created an obstacle for him in this area without our being aware of it.

It could be that the child himself lacks awareness about this issue or has little interest in it or dislikes talking about it.

It is up to us, then, to take the first steps with tact and delicacy, and slowly encourage him to ask questions.

The experience of Sara C. is illustrative: "My boy is not extremely aware in this area. He has many different interests, especially in the scientific field, perhaps an even greater interest than most children his age. He has always asked both my husband and myself many questions on almost any topic. However, his questions about how life begins and about sex were few or practically nonexistent. My task was somewhat difficult because I had to be very alert for the slightest opportunity and use it as an occasion to explain things to him and to complete his education on this subject.

"The first time I began to tell him something was a year or two ago. That seemed to be the proper time, in view of his general maturity.

"One of his aunts had had a baby by caesarean. Phil heard us mention the term. I jumped at the chance to tell him about childbirth and how children are normally born. I added that a caesarean is an exceptional situation because it does not happen naturally but requires an operation to bring the baby out. This was a first step."

*Birth involves motherhood which
should be enhanced by a good
presentation of the facts of life.*

Chapter 2
The Beauty of Motherhood

Respect for womanhood

We have seen how early a child shows interest in childbirth. This brings up the whole question of motherhood.

If we offer explanations of pregnancy, labor, birth, and nursing with the proper attitude, then our children will understand the wonder of womanhood from the very beginning. This is a positive and important value for boys and girls alike. Girls, in particular, will discover the beauty of their own femininity and of their potential to become mothers, and will be preserved from any possible sense of feminine inferiority.

"But when will I have a baby?" asked Clare P., six years old, shortly after speaking with her mother about maternity.

Jennifer I.'s daughter talked about her doll, "She is really my daughter. I love her and carried her inside of me."

Boys learn to value femininity and have respect for it.

"I remember," Mary N. told us, "that when I spoke to Luke about the efforts a mother expends in the birth of her children, he was greatly impressed.

"Later on when we were downtown, he happened to see a woman who was expecting a child. He noticed that she was quite large and he was full of admiration as he exclaimed, 'There's a mother!' and continued with: 'How nice it is to be a mother!' "

Even when it is a question of aesthetics to which many children are quite sensitive, parents should endeavor to enlighten them. "One day when we were at the beach with our girls," related Monica M., "a woman came and sat down under an umbrella nearby, and it was obvious that she was quite large. Claire, the older child, has a strong aesthetic sense. She said to me, almost with a sense of disgust, 'Why is that lady so fat?' I was displeased to hear her talk like that; however, I made no mention of it. Instead I explained how inside that woman, right beneath her heart, a baby was growing. Claire listened attentively, but when I was finished she concluded, 'Yes, maybe so, but she's ugly.' 'That may be true,' I replied, 'but remember that this woman becomes ugly in order to bring a new life to earth. Therefore, during this period, she is really more beautiful than any woman who is not fulfilling this wonderful mission. You should look at her from the point of view of love. You see, a mother gives up her own beauty for love of her baby, to give life to a new person. Therefore she is someone who gives, who loves. When the baby is born she will return to the way she was before.' "

If we present the subject of motherhood well, we can reveal more than just its physical aspect. Other aspects will also become apparent, such as the capacity to suffer, to love, and to live for others.

"With my children, but above all my daughters," said Alice M., "I tried to speak of maternity by emphasizing its greatness, not only from the physical point of view, which in itself is something splendid, but also from the spiritual standpoint.

"When a mother expects a child and feels it come to life, she becomes aware that she is carrying a new person within her because she has collaborated with God in creation. Presenting maternity in this way is very important to me because it enables me to show that this marvelous reality encompasses both the physical and spiritual aspects of human nature."

A new relationship with mother

If the discussion of this topic occurs under favorable circumstances and in a positive way, the relationship between mother and child, whether boy or girl, becomes strong, warm and profound. This marks an exceedingly important moment in the emotional life of the child, in the formation of a balanced psychological outlook. We can almost say that the child begins to understand his ties with his mother as he becomes aware of why he is so attached to her and loves her so much. And at the same time he starts to feel more secure about her love.

It is advisable for mothers to stress the aspect of love, as Marcia P. described. "The twins happened to be present when Larry asked me to explain how babies are formed. As I told him that they are formed inside their mother, I emphasized the aspect of love. I said that God wanted the baby to be close to his mother to create a strong bond of affection between them."

Stages of maternity

When a child makes his first inquiries about babies and learns that they begin life inside their mother, his first desire is to know all he can about this little human being, at first so tiny, who gradually grows larger until he is finally ready to be born. Depending on the age of the child who poses the question and the parents' personal preparation in this field, parents can begin with either of these two points: the egg which becomes fertilized, or the life of the little fetus which forms and develops in the uterus, without any mention of fertilization. Here are some conversations which serve as examples.

Ann Louise B.: "When Laura asked me how the little baby she was looking forward to so anxiously would be born, I replied that every woman has a uterus into which comes the little egg that grows into a child. I showed her a publication that illustrated the growth of a fetus. Every now and then as she watched me grow larger, she went back to look at those illustrations to learn about the stage of the baby's development. I also told her that the baby was part of me and received nourishment through my blood.

"She asked me if the baby suffered when she was resting in my arms and accidentally bumped me. I told her that God has thought of everything: the bag that holds the baby is filled with a liquid that acts as a cushion against bumps and protects him from injuries. It was a beautiful opportunity to talk and reflect on the wonder of nature."

Isabel C.: "When my girls asked me how it can happen that a baby starts to grow in the mother's womb, I told them immediately about the seed that the father gives to the mother. Here because the children were small, I gave only a rudimentary explanation about the mother's egg meeting the father's seed. This develops until it becomes a tiny baby that grows inside her for nine months and nourishes himself through her."

Mary N.: "I have already described how I explained to Luke that babies grow slowly inside their mother for a period of nine months. He was so interested in everything about the life of the fetus during the time of pregnancy that I showed him illustrations in a book on childbirth, which we had in the house. For a long time he studied the various phases of a child's development, how the hands are formed, how the fingers are divided, how the lungs develop. This pleased him tremendously because it appeared to him to be something extraordinary, something miraculous. Then one day he was taking a bath. I had gone into his room a moment for clean underwear. When I returned I saw that he was deeply engrossed. As soon as he realized that I had come back, he said, 'Do you know, mommy, I don't understand why I have this hole in my tummy.' 'It isn't a hole,' I replied, 'it's a little scar. I will tell you how it came to be there. When a baby is still inside his mother, he stays in a sort of bag with walls that stretch slowly as the baby grows. This bag is shaped like a large pear upside down, and it protects the baby so that it can grow peacefully, without danger. But in order to live, a person must eat. A baby inside his mother cannot eat the way you do. Do you remember, when you studied digestion, circulation and respiration a short while ago, how you learned that the food we eat, in order to serve our body, must be transformed into blood, which runs through our body so that every part of it can be nourished? The baby who stays in that bag, which is called a uterus, is connected to the mother's tummy by a cord. His nourishment passes through this cord and, in a sense, he also breathes through it. Naturally, when the baby is born and lives on his own outside his mother, he begins to breath by himself and to drink milk. Therefore, there is no more need for that cord which is cut at the moment of birth, leaving the little scar that everyone has. It is called the umbilical cord.' 'How do they cut it?' 'The doctor uses scissors,' I answered. I realized immediately that his attention was directed toward a problem which is always uppermost in the minds of children: pain. Therefore, while the question was still forming on his lips, I hastened to add, 'However it is not painful, either to the mother or to the baby, because that cord is made of a special skin that doesn't feel pain. It is like cutting finger nails.' He quieted down and seemed satisfied."

How does the baby get out?

When a child has learned all that he wants to know about the life of a baby before he is born, he finally asks the question: "And how does he come out of his mother?" I thought about this question for a while, but since no solution came to me, I asked some other people. Here are a few of their replies:

Mary N. said, "When Luke asked me how a baby comes out of his mother, I found it easy to explain because we had talked about this before. When a baby is ready to be born and his lungs are sufficiently developed and all his other organs are formed, he feels like coming out to begin living on his own. Slowly he starts to push, to find the way out. 'Do you remember,' I told him, 'that I spoke about the bag which is shaped like a pear, the uterus with elastic walls? Well the tip of that pear enlarges naturally. Wait, I'll show you.' I went to find a woolen cap. I put my clenched fists inside it. Then slowly, slowly I opened and separated them, pushing against the sides of the cap, which gradually stretched because of the pressure I exerted. 'Do you see? The baby puts his head near the opening of the bag and then puts it out. Then he puts out his shoulders, his arms, until he is all out. However, you' I added laughingly, 'are so original that you put your feet out first.' 'Yes?' 'Because you jumped around so much when you were still inside of mommy that when it was time for you to come out you were not in the right position.'

"It never occurred to him to ask the location of the external opening of the bag, and so the conversation ended right there."

Isabel C. remarked, "Almost immediately, little girls are interested to know how a baby is born and where it comes out.

"However my children were very young when they asked, and I was afraid that telling them the position might make them confuse the genital apparatus with the urinary apparatus. So I spoke simply of an organ inside every woman, especially designed to receive the fertilized egg and protect it during its development till the moment of birth, when it opens by itself to let the baby come out. Only some time later did I talk about the external opening, and then they asked, 'But does a cut have to be made? Is this why mothers go to the hospital when a baby is born?' 'No,' I replied without hesitation, 'The organ that contains the baby opens by itself. Mothers go to the hospital because care is so important and the baby is so small that sometimes the doctor can be of great help. But many babies are born at home. It is not necessary to go to the hospital.'" Then I explained that this organ is situated in the lower part of the body, and although they may not have noticed, there are two external openings, one for the secretion of urine and the other which leads to the organ that holds the baby and which enlarges at the moment of birth.

"So I was able to discuss personal hygiene with respect to such important organs and how necessary it is to be particularly careful about cleanliness."

Andrew M., the doctor, replied to his children in this manner: "At first the baby is very small. Just think when a baby is born he is only eighteen inches long and weighs only seven pounds. You know how small they are because you have seen babies at the hospital. The mother's body begins preparation many months before. She grows a little larger. If you notice women who expect children, you will see that they walk differently. It is not only because they are larger but also because their frame must change position to make space for the baby. You should know that a baby's head is not made of one piece the way yours is now. It has grooves and is elastic so that it can be squeezed a little smaller. Also, the genital organs of the mother that function in childbirth enlarge little by little until the baby can come out."

As you see, it is not customary for children to ask explicitly where the external opening of the uterus is. They are satisfied that everything happens naturally, as God arranged in his love for this new human being who is coming into the world. But even when this question is asked directly and explicitly, do not be afraid to tell the truth. Here we offer two brief experiences. Carolyn C. told us: "When Frederick was in the first grade, he was playing in our yard one day, when suddenly he stopped and came looking for me. 'Mommy,' he said, 'I just thought of something I wanted to ask you. After the baby grows inside his mother, how does he get out? I tried to think this out for myself, but since I don't think he can get out of the mouth I don't see where he can come out.' I was stunned at first and did not know how to respond. Then I remembered that I had resolved to answer all his questions truthfully. I started by reminding him that his little sister, then two years old, was different from him because the love of God had arranged things that way and I explained the differences in a way that his mind could understand. I concluded by saying that when a baby is ready to be born the part that his little sister has which is different from his own opens naturally to let the baby pass through. At the end, however, I was terrified. I was afraid that I had made a mess of everything, that I had ruined something as beautiful and sacred as birth. But Fred, happy, peaceful and satisfied, simply went back to play. I realized then that I was the one who was not completely free regarding this topic."

Marcia P. said, "From various questions that Larry asked, I realized that he was trying to discover how a baby got out, and that by himself he was unable to come up with a satisfactory solution. Since dialogue between us was always very open and spontaneous, I waited for the matter to mature so that he would ask the precise question. One day he said to me, 'Mommy, I understand where babies come out. They come out from the navel, but why do men have them too?' 'No, Larry,' I explained, 'that is the sign of the cord that connected the baby to his mother and through which he received his nourishment.' Obviously, this was not the place to stop. At that moment, however, I was not yet prepared to answer him, so I let the matter drop and he did not press on either. Later on in the summer we were on vacation and the question came up again. "Well, mommy, tell me where babies come out.' This time it was very easy. I gave a simple explanation. 'You have seen, Larry, that your sisters are different from you, and all women are like your little sisters. They have a sort of door that opens for the babies to come out when they are born.' 'Oh,' he exclaimed, 'now I understand!' He was all excited. This fact created not the slightest problem for him; it seemed the most perfect and logical thing, because he viewed it in all innocence.

The pain of childbirth

When we speak to a child about birth, one of the most frequent problems that arises is pain, a particularly delicate subject for children.

Andrew M., the doctor, related that in trying to make his explanation of the dilation of the birth canal during childbirth more clear and understandable, he said, "Do you remember when your cousin Jackie was born? It took only three hours because Aunt Frances' physical condition made dilation very easy for her. For your mommy it isn't so easy. She always finds it very exhausting. When your brother George was born, it took forty-eight hours and even then forceps had to be used.' 'Did it hurt?' he interrupted, very much concerned. 'Yes.' Then I realized," Andrew concluded, "that the fact that it was painful curbed every bit of his curiosity. He did not speak to me about this for months."

On the same subject, Gloria I. observed: "It is necessary to be careful of 'professional miscalculations' in telling the truth to our children. Frank and I, for example, both being physicians, made some mistakes in answering the first questions. Our children were too young for the explicitly scientific explanations which we gave them. The result was that we stirred up some anxiety in them. We became aware of this when they came to visit me in the hospital soon after their brother was born. The first thing that Elena, the oldest of my children, asked me was this: 'Did you bleed a lot?' because in children's minds the gravity of a situation like this is measured by the quantity of blood lost. We saw that she was very worried. As a result it was necessary for us to calm her and to reassure her."

So parents, especially parents of girls, must decide whether or not to bring up the aspect of pain in birth. The experiences of many parents suggest that it is wiser to deal with this subject and to attempt to explain its true significance.

As Paula R. said to us: "I have always told the truth, and I made no attempt to hide the pain that accompanies childbirth. I tried to explain it by saying that the mother should accept it as something sacred. I spoke of Mary, describing the difficulty, the discomfort and the pain that she had to overcome in order to give Jesus to the world. I did this in order to enable the children to understand the value and importance of suffering, instead of fearing it and shrinking away from it. But most important, I have always tried to explain every human fact in a spiritual light to give it its proper perspective."

This thought was echoed by many mothers:

Grace B. said, "In explaining the various phases of motherhood, I also mention that it does involve some physical pain for the mother. But I add that this is very beautiful because it is like participating in creation. A

mother suffers physically, but Christ suffered too, on the
cross. And together their suffering brings forth a new
creation, a new life.

Alice M. told us: "Certainly I have spoken of the
pain that a mother endures, relating it to Sacred Scrip-
ture and my own experience. By endeavoring to live
always in the present moment pain becomes easy to
endure, because the joy 'that a man has been born into
the world' surpasses the pain. I stressed this point
because I did not want any of the children, especially the
girls, to feel apprehensive about childbirth."

Speaking to children of pain and presenting it in a
positive light, greatly assists in their formation, and
helps them to develop an attitude of love and
selflessness.

"When I told Luke," Mary N. reported, "that cutting the umbilical cord is not painful, other thoughts
came immediately to his mind. He asked if the uterus is
made 'of the thing that doesn't hurt,' trying to find out
whether the movements of the baby cause pain for the
mother. 'No,' I replied frankly, 'in fact when the baby is
ready to be born, the uterus itself contracts and moves in
order to help him get out, which gives the mother some
pains in her stomach. 'Very strong?' he asked. 'Strong
enough,' I said, 'but a mother is content to have them
because a child is being born to daddy and herself, a little
child wanted by God. Soon afterwards, mommy forgets
the physical pain she suffered.' 'Mommy,' Luke interrupted, 'I love you because when I was born I hurt you
and you were happy anyway!'"

To demonstrate just how sensitive children are and
how capable they are of understanding the reality of
birth, we want to relate here in some detail, what hap-

pened to Annmarie and Tom P. during the final period
of her pregnancy with their fifth child, and during the
birth itself.

"When I was expecting our youngest daughter,"
Annmarie told us, "the older children realized that I was
not too well, that it tired me to walk, and I noticed that
they watched me with love and respect. Ann came to me
concerned and said, 'Mommy is it true that when the
baby is born, they will take you to the hospital and cut
you to take him out, that they're going to hurt you?'

" 'No,' I replied, 'it's not true that I will be cut. That
is done only in special situations. Usually when everything is normal, the baby is born by himself, because
nature has taken care of all that. Certainly, the mother
suffers, both while the baby is growing and when he is
born, because he pushes against her. However, it is
beautiful all the same. Anyway, if all goes well I will not
be going to the hospital. The doctor agreed that I could
wait for the baby here at home.' 'Mommy,' Ann interrupted, 'I would like you to tell me when you hurt
because when I know, then I can help you, and that
would make me happy.' 'I'll help you too, mummy,' added
her little brother. 'When you drop something, I'll pick it
up. I'll be glad to do it, because I know it will save you
trouble and I will be doing my share!' "

Tom confided. "In everyone there was an awareness of the event for which we were preparing. It was
no longer something between just the two of us. All of
us shared the anxiety of waiting."

"Then came the moment of birth," Annmarie continued. "During the night, labor pains began and we
called the doctor. Toward eight in the morning we knew
that the baby was almost there. It was Sunday. The

children had slept well all night. I asked Tom to get them up, dress them, and to take them to a neighbor who also had many children. They could all have breakfast and go to church together. When Tom went into their room he found them already awake. Ann heard the doctor arrive and knew something was going on, so she was playing with the little ones so that they would be good and not cause any disturbance. They dressed more quickly and silently than they had ever done before, even helping each other. Then they left without any fuss, or without even insisting on telling me goodbye."

"Our neighbor told me later that during Mass Ann, who knew that I might be suffering, wanted to pray that all might go well.

"As soon as possible, we brought them back home so they could meet their new baby sister. I have never seen the two older children so happy. They felt important because their father and mother had thought them mature enough to participate in this extraordinary event. And they were anxious to know how I was.

"After a few days, when Paula, the newborn, no longer had a little red face and when she had filled out a little, Ann confided to me, 'Do you know, mommy, when she was born I didn't like her, but I told you she was beautiful anyway because I knew you had suffered and I didn't want to disappoint you. But now I really do like her!"

Breast-feeding

The period of breast-feeding offers another opportunity for us to present the wonders of Divine Providence in creating the woman's body in a way that will strengthen the bond of love between a mother and her child.

It is easy to see how nature, designed and created by God, never rushes things: everything happens gradually.

The baby began to live inside his mother, united to her by the umbilical cord, protected and nourished by her. Then he is born and has a life of his own. Yet, he is still not prepared to be dependent and detach himself entirely from the one who has given him life.

He still nourishes himself, though now externally, through her body. Psychological studies concerning the first months of life maintain that this is an important period for the child who is gradually emancipating himself from his mother.

Mary N. related a small episode confirming what we have just said.

"One day, when Luke was about four years old, he had occasion to watch a mother breast-feeding her baby. He was very interested and it pleased him greatly when I explained what was happening. He wanted to know if he too, as a baby, had been fed like that. I explained that since I had not had enough milk, I had fed him from the bottle. He seemed a little disappointed, but then asked, 'But you did hold me in your arms?' He instinctively needed to be assured that he had not missed out on my love and care. 'Certainly, I held you in my arms.' 'And the milk was good like milk from a mommy?' 'Yes,' I replied, 'it was very good. You liked it so much that you always wanted more than you were supposed to have.' He smiled, and seemed happy and content."

From the very beginning, a child should learn the difference between the sexes.

Chapter 3
The Opposite Sex

Anatomical differences

It is good for children, even from a very early age, to have occasion to see children of the opposite sex and notice the anatomical characteristics that make them different from each other.

"In large families this happens very easily," as Alice M., like many other mothers, related, "because many occasions arise spontaneously when a family includes both boys and girls."

The most common instance is bathing the new-born baby, an event of great interest to all the children in the family. But also in families where there is only one child or children of only one sex, it is good to seek natural opportunities to provide this experience for the children.

Isabel C. told us: "My daughters grew up in very close contact with their boy cousins. My sister-in-law used to leave them with little or no clothing on at times during the summer when it was extremely hot. Therefore, Ida and Louise became aware of the differences almost immediately, without having the least problem."

Esther G. said, "Having only girls, I thought it wise to take them to my friend's house to see her new baby boy. Sometimes we saw him bathed and changed."

At first children do notice these sexual differences,

but do not ask the reason for them. Just as girls wear skirts and boys wear pants, or have their hair cut differently (not always these days), so also do they have distinctive physical characteristics.

As Esther G. told us: "When our girls noticed that boys were not just like them, they asked me, 'Why are they different?' Since they were very young, I used to reply, 'Because they are boys and you are girls.' I marveled at their acceptance of this reply, which seems to say nothing, but for them was enough."

So also children see numerous varieties of animals, but never ask why there are so many species. In fact, they appreciate the variety. Like six-year-old Charles, they lament the lack of variety in the human species. We could not help laughing when Alice M. told us: "The other day Charles, who was seated eating nuts while I was working in the kitchen, began a profound discussion with me. He said, 'Mommy, you and I are really different, aren't we? You are a woman and I am a man. But why are there only two kinds? There are many kinds of animals: there are cows, horses, birds, dogs and so on. But for us there are only men and women.'"

Children often associate this anatomical difference with the excretion of urine. It is better, however, not to anticipate, but to wait until they ask precise questions about how the baby emerges at birth or, later on, about fertilization. As Esther G. affirmed: "At the beginning I did not feel that it was the proper time to say more. But now that I have explained all the organs and ducts and even fertilization to my girls, everything seems logical to them. They understand what it means, physiologically speaking, to be a man and to be a woman."

This awareness of the two sexes, even though

superficial, becomes useful later on because it leads more easily and naturally to fuller explanations. Indeed, as children become more mature, they discover the anatomical differences between adults, and the situation becomes more challenging. This is generally the time when children become more aware of their sexuality and begin to identify more consciously than ever before with their father or mother.

As we have already said, we must help our children to discover God's providential design for femininity and masculinity. This means explaining how male and female organs relate to each other and have a life-giving function.

The experiences of Brian and Marcia P. in this regard were very interesting. Marcia told us: "When we were on vacation at the beach, Larry noticed the differences between men and women and shared his thoughts with me: 'Men are made like this... and women are made like this...' We talked together for a while about this."

"However," said Brian, "at that time we didn't go any further with it. But I remember how later on, he woke up early, one morning and came to find us still in bed. All of a sudden after a moment of thought he said to Marcia, 'Are you different from daddy?' 'Certainly,' she replied. 'I am a woman, I am the mother; and daddy is a man like you.' 'Yes,' he said, convinced and summed things up by naming all the various organs. Some time later, in my studio in New York, he saw a drawing of one of the few nudes I had done."

"Yes," continued Marcia, "it was a female figure, a study. I saw Larry looking at it and asked him, 'Do you like it? Daddy drew it.' Larry was engrossed for a moment and then explained the whole figure to us, one part after another, as if to clarify his understanding." "What I liked about his explanation," remarked Brian, "was that it showed a positive awareness. The breast, for example, he defined as the 'part for milk.' He recognized in that female figure a mother, a woman with a maternal function." At this moment Brian went on to confide: "In the past I had been very concerned, not so much over my drawings or even my nude studies themselves as at my public showings. I used to first make a careful selection of works to be shown. I would say, 'No, not this one; it didn't turn out quite right. I would examine every one and only when they were beyond reproach would I show them. The drawing Larry saw had been shown. Since it had passed my rigorous standards, I was content to let him see it. And now this very drawing, made years before, was helping him to clarify his ideas. The fact that I, his father, had drawn that figure gave him, with his strong aesthetic sense, the courage to take a pencil and draw a woman, with all her female characteristics, and a man, with his. From that day, it was as if his tensions were released. He no longer asked questions on this subject because, evidently, he had resolved the problem himself."

Modesty and self-restraint

Discussion of the anatomical differences between man and woman leads us to the matter of modesty and self-restraint.

The question arises: is it good to instill modesty and reserve in children when they are still so young and innocent? Parents have offered some sensible replies.

"I deliberately left Larry and his twin sisters together quite often," related Marcia P., "until I knew they were aware of their physical differences. Then, subtly I began to instruct them about modesty."

Alice M. suggested: "I think it is important to teach children very early about self-restraint and modesty, even if these values seem to be going out of style. But I want to emphasize that it must be done simply and with discretion so as to create a wholesome balance between spontaneity and reserve, taking into account the age and sensitivity of each individual child."

Esther G. noted how important it is to avoid drawing undue attention to particular postures and attitudes, as this could create a problem when there is none. "I always tried not to call attention to actions which are normal for children, for example, innocent exposure. I have all girls and I felt that it was important for them to be neat, modest and dignified. However, I always pretended not to notice little indiscretions. Instead, I tried to distract them, to keep them busy and show real respect for their natural behavior, so simple and innocent. Eventually the matter took care of itself, perhaps because they had noticed how I myself behave. They learned spontaneously in this area as in others, I think, from practical daily experience."

Other people whom we interviewed insisted that modesty is instinctive. For example, Mary N. observed: "From my own experience, I have learned that modesty is a problem which never exists during a child's earliest years. Later on, if a child is normal, modesty is instinctive; a child becomes reserved even in front of his mother."

Marcia P. offered this comment: "One might think

that an open, candid sex education, such as the one we have tried to give, might result in a lack of concern for modesty and reserve. Instead, we have had precisely the opposite experience.

"Little girls, for example, have a strong sense of modesty. We always go to the seaside for our vacation, where everything is out in the open. We live in a city decorated with billboards of every kind. Yet the girls, even if they only want to change their skirts, do not want their brother around nor do they want anyone in the house to see them. They must have an innate sensitivity, as I can say in all honesty, we have never had to tell them: 'You should be ashamed. Pull your hem down. Behave yourself and act like a lady.'"

Attraction to the opposite sex

From their very first days, children have a sexual instinct, and feel attracted toward the opposite sex. Naturally there is a whole range of ways in which this instinct and reaction to the opposite sex is expressed, depending on the age and the temperament of the child.

Often boys begin by being in love with their mothers. Since they cannot immediately emancipate themselves from the one who gave them life, they remain attached to her by a special emotional bond. Besides, his mother is the first female figure with whom a boy comes in contact. Girls, on the other hand, undergo a fascination with the first male figure in their lives, their father.

"When he was about five, Larry went through a phase of being in love with his mother," said Marcia P., "and began to develop a strong jealousy toward his father. Often he would say to me with great irritation, 'Why did daddy get here first? Why did he marry you? I wanted to marry you? Now whom will I marry when I grow up?' I remember one summer when we were on vacation at the ocean. Early in the morning Larry, still half asleep, was fantasizing or actually dreaming. Then, when I went in to say 'good morning' to him, he said, 'Mommy, I was thinking of you all dressed in flowers. You were beautiful!' Or: 'I thought of you all dressed like a bride, with a long white veil.' I tried not to assign any special importance to these comments or to be severe with him, but rather to lessen his dependence on me gradually so that it would not cause any psychological problem."

As Marcia P. has noted, this phase during which the child idealizes the maternal figure as the only female figure, or the paternal figure as the only male figure, can last for some time.

Then finally the child begins his own social experiences. He discovers boys and girls his own age, and makes choices on the basis of his personal preferences."

Marcia P. continued her conversation: "During the winter Larry went to nursery school. It was there in the school environment that he became aware of girls. One day he came home and said to me, 'Mommy, I saw Laura. Do you know, she has two braids and is very pretty. I like her a lot!' A few days later, he brought up the subject again. He was almost angry. 'Mommy, I'm afraid that Laura is going to be prettier than you!' The change had taken place. In fact, a short while later he announced to me, 'When I am grown up, I will marry her. She is my girlfriend. I wish I could give her a ring.'"

At this point in their lives, boys and girls both

begin to react to the vague feelings arising within them.
If they have good relationships with their parents and,
above all, if the parents do not ridicule these disclosures,
the children will open up to talk and reflect on their
behavior and thus mature more easily.

Here are two experiences that demonstrate this.
The first is from Marcia P.:

"In the first grade Larry met the same little girl he
had seen at nursery school. He immediately told me
about it. 'Oh, yes,' I replied. 'Did you say hello to her?'
'No,' he replied at once. 'I didn't say anything to her, not
even hello. In fact, when I see her I act silly and even fall
down. Do you know,' he continued a little while later,
'my teacher sent me to Laura's class with a notice, but
outside the door, I had to take a deep breath because my
heart was pounding.'"

Mary N. said, "When Luke was in third grade on
one of the first days of school, I went to wait for him at
the door of the church where the children had gone for
the opening Mass of the school year. The children were
out in the church yard, laughing, shoving, and joking
around.

"Luke was with a group from his class, teasing
some girls, probably from another class.

"When Luke saw me he came over. I took him by
the hand and asked 'What were you saying to those
girls?' 'We were teasing them, of course.' 'Why?' I asked
innocently. 'We always do it,' he replied, 'and we call
them all kinds of names. On the way out of school when
we pass their corridor, we always do it, too! They make
believe that they're angry, but I know that they like it!'
Because I looked surprised, he added an explanation.
'Yes, we tease them and make believe we don't like

them, but do it to get their attention and impress them. We would be embarrassed to let them know, so we act like that.'

"I did not make any comment about this explanation because I was so surprised at his ability to view the whole business with such objectivity, and to be so aware of the actual situation. However, I was very pleased that he had felt so free to tell me about it."

Children mature one step further when they discover and appreciate the attributes and qualities of the opposite sex.

We asked Tina, six years old, "Why do you want George to be your boyfriend?" She replied, "Because he is stronger than anybody else." When we asked Ruth, a seven year old, a similar question, she replied, "When we come out of school, he wants to carry my books and when we have a race, he comes in first.

"In August we went to Cape Cod because Brian had an exhibition of paintings," Marcia told us, as she described this new phase of her son's life. "In the house where we were staying there was a little girl, the landlady's daughter. She was a year or so older than our son and was very polite and well mannered. She took a liking to Larry, and during the course of our stay she often prepared him treats and just generally showed him kindness and attention. As a result, I believe that Larry discovered femininity through her. When we returned home, he drew some posters which proclaimed, 'Adriana is very beautiful' and he delegated the twins to parade around the house with them."

As a child approaches adolescence, he begins to feel a desire for someone who is not just attractive, but who notices and appreciates him, who understands and listens to him, someone whom he can trust, but someone outside his own family and his own sex. Instinctively, a child seeks psychological, emotional and intellectual characteristics complementary to his own. This is a difficult period because during adolescence sexual maturity is as rapid as physical development, and this creates many problems for children and parents alike.

It is a difficult time. Parents must subtly make themselves more available than ever but without imposing. Children, because of their ardent search for independence, are often unaware of their need for parental guidance. Temptations are strong, and children must learn to deal with them, as they must learn to struggle with a host of conflicting impulses.

Esther G. recalled the time her eldest daughter told her she wanted to go around with a group of girls and boys because many of her classmates were always speaking about their boyfriends. But at the same time, her daughter had confided, she was a little scared by this desire.

"So I had to explain to her," said Esther, "that these feelings are normal. From childhood on we have the desire to meet someone who can be our companion, whom we can marry and then become a mother. This desire becomes stronger as we mature. 'And you,' I told her, 'feel this need strongly. Things happen that you never expected. But this is fine; it means that you are a normal girl.' I explained all this to her to remove any sense of guilt. But then I added, 'On the other hand it is precisely because the union between man and woman is something so profound and beautiful that it is necessary to wait for the proper moment. You have to wait so you don't spoil everything. You see, rather than repressing this feeling you should guard it as a treasure within you. All the things God has given us are good and beautiful and have a good purpose. However, if we are not careful, we can ruin them and use them unwisely.'"

Physiological development of the sexes

"Chris, our older daughter, developed very early," Esther G. told us. "She was not yet eleven when she began to show signs of physical development. I reassured her by saying, 'You see, you are beginning to develop. You are beginning to become a woman.' However, I had never imagined that it would happen so soon, and as a result I was almost caught by surprise. I had intended to discuss the subject in depth with her and explain the physiological aspects of womanhood. But when menstruation began, I had still not had a talk with her. I had waited too long and felt bad about it. Fortunately, this experience had no negative effects on Chris, because there was a close bond between us. Yet it did serve to warn me about preparing my other children. I realized I had made a mistake and so I had a talk with the others before it was too late.

"I spoke with each child individually about this, and I noticed how it deepened our relationship, which I think we really needed."

Yes, it is very important to prepare children of both sexes for the change that will take place.

Martha S. told us: "My daughter, who is only nine years old, is a very precocious and active girl, so I have already had a talk with her. I informed her that at a certain age girls undergo changes. For example, I ex-

plained that there are glands especially designed to
supply milk and that they develop and enlarge to form
the breasts. For her this was a discovery, because even
though she knew about breast-feeding, she had never
imagined that breasts develop in every woman as early
as puberty. I also explained that the female body contains many other glands and organs that develop as a
girl becomes an adolescent and finally a woman. I spoke
of the ovaries, which contain the eggs for fertilization,
that can start a new life when united with the seed from
the father. At this time, I explained the menstrual cycle,
saying that it sometimes involves a little pain, weariness
or discomfort, but that it is all quite normal and easy to
cope with. Laura listened very attentively to me; she
displayed no anxiety, but rather great love.

"Since this discussion touched on the male anatomy, I compared the male development with that of the
female. But the male description was naturally more
general, since I was speaking to a girl."

Isabel C. told us: "Ida told me that she felt a twinge
in one part of her breast. She also noticed that some hair
was growing and she asked me the reason. I was glad for
the opportunity to tell her that she was beginning to
become a young woman. 'Your breast twinges, as you
say, because you are growing up,' I said. You notice it on
one side because both sides do not always develop simul-
taneously. Breasts function when we are mothers, you
know, to provide milk for the baby.' I had already told
her about the mammary glands. She enjoyed our talk. It
seemed to her that this development was a step toward
motherhood. I then explained that hair grows on different parts of our body, as protection for organs or delicate areas. I pointed out, for example, how hair covers

the head, and how eyelashes and eyebrows protect the eyes. 'As you become an adult,' I added, 'very delicate and very important organs begin to develop and so hair begins to grow near them.'

"This provided an opportunity to describe more fully the genital organs of the woman and to say something also about those of the man.

"It was at this time that I told her about menstruation and pointed out what it means so that when it happened she would not feel the same sense of disgust that I had felt because of lack of preparation. I helped her realize what sacrifice is all about, and while it is an inconvenience for a woman it is something very positive. It seemed to me that she accepted everything very well."

Other mothers had stressed another very important fact: it is necessary to speak also of the development of the opposite sex. This has already been mentioned in the experiences just reported, but Alice M. and Mary N. dealt with it explicitly.

As Alice M. confided: "I spoke to our girls about their development when they were about ten. First, I described their physiology and its function, and then, started with the anatomical differences, I went on to discuss the male physiology and its function. In a similar way, I talked to our son Mark about female physiology, about its beauty and harmony. I was also able to explain in particular the perfection and the regularity of the menstrual cycle. His reaction to our conversation was so positive that he declared, 'Just think how God planned everything.'"

Mary N. related the following: "One day Luke asked me at what age he would become an adult, and how would he know. With my husband's help, I discussed male development, beginning with a description of the genital organs and their functions.

" 'You know that glands play a very important role in the human body. In the small organs on either side of the penis, there are two small glands called testicles. These glands are special because they send a very useful substance into the blood so it can be carried through the whole body. But they also produce the sperm cells, a group of very small seeds call spermatozoa, which generate life.

" 'When a boy is about to become a man, these glands begin to work very actively: the testicles begin to produce sperm. When a boy begins to grow a beard and his voice deepens, it means he is becoming a man and will be able to produce life.'

"However, I did not succeed as I had hoped in telling him precisely what goes on during female development and the outward changes that accompany it.

"One day he was watching a children's program on television and saw an ad for diapers. Luke left his place in front of the TV and came to me. 'In the bathroom,' he said, 'I saw some things like that. Why do we still have them in the house? Are they left over from when I was a baby?' 'No,' I replied, 'they are another kind that mothers use.

" 'Do you remember when I told you that sometimes when the egg leaves the mother's ovary it meets the seed from the father and is fertilized, with the result that a baby is born? And do you remember that during the nine months the baby remains within the mother's uterus, he is nourished by means of a cord? Well, a woman's egg leaves the ovary every twenty-eight days. But before the egg leaves, the uterus collects many nutritive substances so that the egg will be able to receive nourishment and grow if it fertilized.

" 'If the egg does not meet the father's seed those nutritive substances are no longer of use, so they leave the uterus in the form of blood.

" 'Women use napkins (which do look a little like children's diapers) to absorb this blood.' At this point I added that this flow of blood happens not only to mothers but to all women and even to girls, from the time they develop into young women at ten to fourteen years of age. Because all women are capable of becoming mothers, just as all men are capable of becoming fathers.'

"Here I stressed the ultimate purpose of male and female development: fatherhood and motherhood. It seems to me that knowing not only how the opposite sex is made, but also how their body functions, may help children, especially boys, to avoid developing an obsessive curiosity about the body of the opposite sex.

Psychological development and the crisis of puberty

"If it is necessary," continued Mary N., "to prepare children for their physical development, it is no less important to speak with them about all of the impulses, desires and moods that are part of adolescence, the growing period. My husband and I have tried to speak with our children about these things, because we realized that while we could not eliminate the so-called puberty crisis, we could help the children know what to expect so they would be better prepared to deal with it successfully."

Esther G. also talked about this difficult period of life. "The puberty crisis is real! With plenty of frustration and tears! We watched the children suffer, and felt there was absolutely nothing we could do about it. However, I had forewarned Chris and this was of some help. And almost every evening I would spend some time with her to give her a chance to talk and unload some of the things that weighed on her mind and troubled her.

"So I think the crisis was resolved rather quickly and without the rebellion that often characterizes this stage in life."

The ultimate question: the male role in procreation

This is the ultimate question, the one that most of us fear when we try to encourage dialogue and answer truthfully our children's first questions on "how babies are born". We are afraid the first question will be: "What makes a baby start growing inside the mother?" "How does the father's seed unite with the mother's egg?"

But while children deal with all the issues we have been discussing, they never actually raise this particular question. Why do they not ask about the father's role in the birth of a child and what makes the children his? Because children have a high spiritual concept of motherhood and fatherhood which goes far beyond a purely physical approach. Daddy works, he takes care of his wife and children, he protects and sustains his family

and he knows how to get things done. This expresses an
exalted notion of fatherhood.

As a result they hardly ever think of children being
born outside the constituted family, that is outside
marriage.

"I was amazed by the fact," said Rose T., "that even
after I had told Sandra explicitly that unmarried men
and women can become mothers and fathers and that
men and women have natural attractions towards one
another, and after I had described how fertilization
occurs, she asked me one day when she heard some talk
about an unwed mother, "But how can a baby be born if
it doesn't have a father and if a woman doesn't have a
husband?'"

All that has been said should reassure us that no
matter at what age a boy asks about the male role in
procreation, if he got through the other issues calmly
and serenely, he will be prepared to accept our answer
to this question as well. Of course our answer, while
always respecting the truth, will be tailored to the
maturity of the child.

It would seem helpful to give some actual experiences of this matter, just as we have been doing all
along.

"During my third pregnancy," explained Alice M.,
"Laura, who by now was growing up, asked how babies
form inside the mother. Laura was often with me when
I bathed my second child and when I changed him. So
she was aware of the differences between men and
women. She remembered that as a woman has the uterus with the egg, a man has a supply of seed. One of
these seeds, if it contacts an egg, may generate a child.

The different physical makeup of men and women serves precisely for this purpose. I showed her a key and explained it like this: 'It is like putting a key into a lock. When mommy and daddy think they would like to have a child the father puts his seed with the mother's egg so a baby can be formed."

Martha S. said, "One day my daughter asked, 'Mommy, one day you told me that the daddy gives the seed to the mommy. How does he do it?'

"So I explained how it happens. I told her about the physical attraction of man and woman. And I explained that it is from this attraction, from this love that children are born. Since I had briefly explained male anatomy to her, I now told her that the male organ enters the female one to deposit the seed."

Isabel C. stated: "When Ida asked me how the male seed can reach the egg in order to fertilize it, I said, 'You have seen that your cousin Greg's body is not like yours. There is a reason. Greg's external organ makes him different from you, and this is very important. It has a kind of passageway to let out the fertilizing seeds that form within a man. It places the seeds in the female organ. Therefore it must be kept clean and healthy."

Esther G. said, "After having asked how babies are born and where they get out, Carol asked me, 'How does the baby get inside the mother?' I confess that at that moment I did not know what to say. It was obvious that I was not ready for this, so I said, 'Look, this is a very great and beautiful mystery. Mommy, daddy and God all work together. I will tell you all about it one of these days.

"Immediately, however, I made a point of talking with mothers who were better prepared than myself and in whom I could have confidence. A friend of mine recommended a book, *The Mystery of Life Explained to the Young*, which was truly a help. It is in two volumes, one with sketches and illustrations for the children themselves to read. The only thing it does not have is the explanation of the act itself, which is left for the parents themselves to explain. After she read the book, Carol came and asked me again: 'We understand everything, except what the father does. How does he put the seed inside the mother?' This time I did not dodge; I spoke my piece.

"I will try to repeat what I said, but it is hard to recall it exactly, since the intimate atmosphere that developed helped me find words in a way I never expected.

"I began by saying that men and women marry because they love each other. They unite in their love and from this union a child is born. But how does this happen? Here, I explained in a natural and simple way how the male organ is made, how, when the father and mother come together in love, the father deposits his seed in the womb of the mother, and how this seed unites with the egg to generate a new life.

"While I was explaining this, I saw that the girls took in everything I said and were enthralled. It all developed so naturally and turned out to be as easy for them to accept as it was for me to explain. They were not disturbed at all. I noticed how innocent they were. Evil had not touched them. They had no bad experiences. It was all very beautiful for them, because it became clear to them how father and mother worked hand in hand with God. Husband and wife love each other and can bring forth a child, but the creative intervention of

God is also necessary. The child's soul is given not by the parents, but by God. So the greatest thing of all is the part God plays."

Here is the experience of Sandra C. "A short time ago, while were were speaking about the birth of a child, Paul made this observation: 'If children are born from the mother, what does the father have to do with it?' I had at home a small booklet written especially for children, very simple but satisfactory, and I gave it to him to read. I explained that a child can be born only from the love of a father and mother. From the booklet he learned that the father participates in conception, because the male seed is necessary for procreation. It gave no further details, and I did not add any because it did not seem like the proper time. In fact, this was enough to satisfy Paul. The fundamental concept that remained with him was that a baby is born as a result of the love between father and mother.

"Later on, during the summer, Paul asked me how the seed gets into the mother's womb. I explained that not all love is the same, but it is always beautiful. And I compared for him the different types of love here on earth. Then I told him that between husband and wife there is a special love, one that brings them close and makes them very affectionate toward each other. While they are close and expressing their love, the father feels the seed leave and enter the mother's womb, where it can form a new life. I tried to impress on him that everything happens in a relationship of love."

Often when children get to the point of talking about fertilization and how it occurs, they hesitate to ask the question. Therefore, it is most important for parents to be attentive and observant.

As Marcia P. told us: "Now Larry knows almost everything. The only question that has not yet come up is that of the father's role. Since Larry is an alert, logical and precocious child, he may already be wondering. Till now he has been so free and open with us, that I am surprised he has not brought it up. If he waits any longer to ask this final question, I think I will have to raise it. I want to be sure there is not some slight obstacle holding him back."

That is certainly a possibility. When the time comes to ask about fertilization (and this should happen by age twelve) children are already becoming young men and women. Many outside contacts and influences have already begun to affect their relationship with us and they sense that this question is not like the others. They may no longer have the simplicity and innocence they had when they asked how babies are born just as they asked about thunder in a storm. More often than not they have already had to overcome small trials and temptations. And in their relationship with us, even though our rapport may be the best, they may find themselves ill at ease. So we have to meet them half way and help them when they fail to ask explicit questions.

"With Mark it was like this," said Alice M. "One evening this summer he could not get to sleep and he told me that for some time he had had difficulty falling asleep. The next morning, since we happened to sleep in the same room that night I said to him, 'Perhaps something is on your mind,' 'No, not at the moment,' he replied, 'but for a while...' And he began to open up We got into a discussion and we were able to go quite far. I told him about fertilization. As soon as I men-

tioned the word, he exclaimed, 'Oh, just like the flowers.' And it was that simple. In fact, when he asked me
how fertilization occurs, I described it for him, and went
into male and female physiology, giving him a more
detailed and complete account than I had done before.

"Then I spoke of a 'marital embrace,' so that he
might understand that this was an important aspect of
love and not merely a physical thing. Mark asked me,
with unusual innocence for a boy of his age, 'Does this
happen only once in a lifetime?' 'No,' I responded. 'It
happens many times, naturally and with great spontaneity. It is necessary for each child that is born.' And
then, since I had already explained the menstrual cycle, I
was able to bring up the subject of contraceptives which
interrupt ovulation and impede conception. I was able
to explain the position of the Church and the teaching
of the papal encyclical, *Humanae Vitae*. Our discussion
became an important and beautiful dialogue, in which
we were able to view sexuality in the context of a full
human life that included even the spiritual side. Everything made sense. We spoke of the importance of chas-
tity for young people before they marry and I explained
that special preparation is necessary before marriage, so
that one knows he cannot just do as he pleases in marriage without taking into account the other person,
because every human action, especially for a Christian, is
based on love. I also spoke of virginity, of those who do
not marry because they accept the invitation of Jesus, in
the Gospel, to remain virgins for the Kingdom of
Heaven and to belong totally to God. I said that both
matrimony and virginity are beautiful vocations even if
the second is greater, and that everything is in the hands
of God, and to God one road is as good as the other. The

best thing for him to do would be what God calls him to. I added that from the human point of view, marriage might seem richer and more complete because God has created us male and female to complement one another, but virgins can also reach fulfillment through deep spiritual relationships, based on genuine love for others.

"Mark seemed to understand everything perfectly and was quite happy and content."

Sexuality which is not governed by the spiritual and moral order leads to chaos instead of personal fulfillment.

Chapter 4
Sexuality and the Moral Order

Sexual instinct

"Even if they have no evil intent, children do have their natural instincts and are aware of them from a very early age. That is something to think about!" observed Martha S.

This is so true. We cannot wait until our children are grown before we concern ourselves with the dangers they may encounter, the vices they may adopt, and the influences to which external pressures may subject them.

If it is of the utmost importance to have a continuously open relationship with our children so they will feel free to ask their questions; it is even more vital that this relationship give them the possibility of selecting us as the ones in whom they want to confide. "I remember," said Mary N., "an incident that happened some years ago and which remained a focal point in my relationship with Luke. It was late one spring evening. Luke and I were home alone because my husband was away on business. To make things pleasant for him, I set a small table for supper on the terrace. Luke noticed that this was special and showed his appreciation. We began to eat with a great sense of closeness between us.

"On a terrace nearby, children were playing.

"Suddenly Luke said to me, 'Do you see that girl in

the blue skirt?' He hesitated a moment, then continued, 'I like her a lot. I always see her when I go to piano lessons. She has blue eyes.' I became aware that this was a very important moment in our relationship. I was afraid of destroying his confidence or of somehow breaking the mood that had been created between us. Therefore, I decided to remain silent and, with the most natural and relaxed attitude possible, to wait for him to go on.

"Certainly, I never expected to hear the disclosures that followed. Luke said nothing for a moment. Then, as if continuing a conversation that he had already begun, he said, 'One of my friends at school says that he is engaged. He told me that one time when they were at the beach together he peeked through the keyhole and saw his girlfriend undressed. He asked me if I had seen mine. Then he said that if I wanted to we could sneak into his father's store and look at some magazines with pictures of nude women.' He heaved a sigh as if a great weight had been removed. I waited a little before asking, 'What do you think?' 'I think nude women are ugly,' he replied. 'Women, as God has made them, are not ugly but beautiful,' I told him, 'because He made them capable of becoming mothers. But you realize, even if you don't know how to explain it, that the reason men picture them like that in magazines is not good, and you are right. What did you say to your friend?' 'That I wasn't interested! But then, especially when I go to bed, I get bad thoughts and I don't feel good. I didn't want to tell you because I am ashamed. But now I'm glad I did tell you so you can help me.' He was nearly crying. I was uneasy. Without letting it show, I tried to find out what these thoughts of his were. He told me many things, at first laboriously, but then, seeing that I was not shocked, more and more freely. But I was completely in the dark, because I did not know if the things he was telling me were normal. What did I know about things that tempt boys? And my husband was away. I thought it was important for me to calm Luke down. I tried to lessen his fears by telling him that thoughts like these probably come to everyone, children and adults alike. He could ease his mind by telling me about them, or by talking to his father or his confessor, and then relax. 'It is enough if you don't want them and if you don't dwell on them when they come,' I advised him.

"My husband and I agreed that for a while I should stay with Luke on some pretext or other until he went to sleep. In a short time the problem had practically disappeared. But the most positive result of the incident is that every time something comes up he comes to tell us and this gives him a lot of peace."

Martha S. was one of several persons who related a similar experience. "Some months ago, Lucy and I were alone together for some reason I do not remember. We had just sat down to supper, when she said, 'You know, mom, I am really upset, I'm really...' She had difficulty explaining her feelings. 'Why?' I asked. 'Because I can't get out of my mind the picture of an unclothed man and woman embracing each other.' I felt my blood rise. I was stunned. As a young girl I had never had thoughts like these and was not sure if they were normal for a child of nine. Nevertheless, I gathered the courage to ask her, 'But why? How come? Did you see something that bothered you?' 'No,' she replied with certainty, I have not seen anything. It is a temptation. I think about it and see it even when I go to bed.' I did my best to keep calm and let her open up.

"That evening when she went to bed I went to her room because I thought she might be disturbed. In the light reflected from the hallway I could see her stretched out in bed with her eyes wide open in the dark. We prayed together. At the end, tired and exhausted, she fell asleep. In time, with the help I could give her, her problem slowly disappeared.

"What impressed me was the certainty with which Lucy recognized that it was a temptation."

And yet, it is no wonder. Even when they are very young and without evil intent, children immediately realize when they are doing, thinking or desiring something which is not good for them. If they are able to talk to us about it, we are in a good position to ease their conscience and help them to regain their peace of mind.

Outside influences

Children are exceedingly sensitive to outside influences: conversations, bad example, illustrations, photographs and so on.

"For sensitive children with lively minds, visual impressions can present a particular problem," observed Anthony M. "Our Chris, for example, is very observant of the world around her. Some of the strongest influences are advertisements for movies and consumer products."

It is precisely the most sensitive children who realize their own vulnerability and overreact.

We have collected several experiences that relate to this problem.

Martha S. said, "One day Lucy and I were walking down the street and saw a wall poster. As I remember, it was an ad for bath soap. There was a woman scantily and revealingly dressed. Nearby there was a man observing her. Lucy saw the ad and said almost in anger, 'See those two? Boy, are they stupid!'

"She was upset, but telling me about it helped free her. Realizing that sensitivity and sexuality awaken at an early age, I was very glad that she was open enough about it so I could help her."

Marcia P. stated: "Our son is quite sensitive. Perhaps it is just part of being a boy. Suggestive scenes in newspapers and magazines and on television make a real impression on him. I became aware of this one day when we were downtown together and I stopped to buy a magazine. Larry stopped to look at the covers of some of the magazines. I noticed when we were leaving that he turned around to take another look. I thought immediately that I should not let those ideas remain with him, so I asked him, 'Do you want a comic book? Come on, we'll go look at one. Was there something special that you wanted to see?' He turned around, furious. He was really and truly angry. His face was flushed the whole time he was answering me: 'Did you see that fool? She is really crazy to let herself be photographed like that. Have you ever seen such stuff?' He was alluding to a woman who was practically nude. He could hardly find words strong enough to express his indignation. I became concerned to try to control his feelings, which were almost hateful. 'Listen, Larry,' I said, 'first of all you must realize that the woman probably grew up in a family with little upbringing. Who knows what kind of life she has had? We should try to understand, although this doesn't change the fact that she is doing wrong. Would you ever think of seeing your mother photographed like that?' 'Never, it's horrible!' 'And yet people who want to make a lot of money selling magazines take advantage of this type of person, because people like to look at them.' I went on to talk to him about our instincts, but in a simple way because he was so young."

Mary N. related this experience. "We were at the beach one summer, staying in a cottage. Luke and I were alone one day because my husband had gone to the city. We were walking along the beach, talking as we strolled. Luke, who was ahead of me, turned around suddenly and said, 'I saw some advertising signs and I don't understand why they are so stupid. There was a naked woman, covered only with one little strip. On it was the name, Beatrice. They want to sell bathing suits and they don't even show one, just the trade mark. And pictures like that make me nervous!' The whole time he was talking, he was excited and flushed. I thought that perhaps he was waiting for my judgment. At any rate, he continued, letting down his barrier of reserve.

"'It makes me mad because I know I should not look, but yet I enjoy looking. This happens with a lot of pictures, like movie ads. I don't want to look at these pictures, but I look at them anyway.' 'It's something very normal,' I told him calmly. 'All boys, and others too, find themselves in your situation.' I was happy that he could talk to me about it, and that I could explain how things are, because I know how dangerous it is when children of this age begin to think they are hopelessly evil. 'The fact is, it's natural,' I continued. 'Divine Providence planned it that to create new life a man and a woman should be joined together, just as we need to eat, drink and sleep in order to live and stay healthy. So God connected a pleasure with these vital necessities to make it easier to do them. We must eat, so God has given us hunger. We must sleep, so God has given us weariness. In the same way, man must unite with woman, and God has given them spontaneous attraction toward one another. These urges, that is, these instincts are all good because they were placed in human nature by God, and everyone experiences them. But people do not always use them well, that is, in moderation and according to the will of God. For example, to be hungry and to eat is good, but if out of gluttony you try to get the most possible pleasure you can from eating, and stuff yourself to the limit or eat things that make you sick, then you are not doing it to preserve the gift of life that God has given you. You are endangering that life and so it is wrong.

"'Because the instinct that men and women have for each other is so strong, it is particularly difficult for them to remain faithful to the will of God. Sometimes we go so far as to say that human beings are slaves of their instincts and their passions. They are no longer in control of themselves when they are at the mercy of their instincts. Some people do not have the slightest interest in God, in his will, or the order he has established. What do they do? They exploit and stir up people's instincts in order to sell products. Because you are attracted by that picture, without being aware of it, you select the product or go to the movie advertised. Do you understand?' 'Yes, but it doesn't seem like a very good thing.' 'Do you know why you become angry when you see that kind of illustration?' He looked at me anxiously, because he did not think it possible that his solution could be so near at hand. 'Because you understand that pictures like that take away your freedom; they make you a slave. This loss of freedom is repugnant to everyone because it is the greatest gift that God could have given us.

"'Women who wish to live right and not lead others to evil do not go around half undressed, nor do they allow themselves to be photographed like that. And they know that, too, deep in their own hearts.

"'When people were living in Paradise, they were in a state of innocence and felt no need to cover themselves, because instincts were as God had created them before they had been corrupted. But after the first sin, the bible tells us the first people were ashamed to be nude and felt it necessary to cover themselves with fig leaves.' 'Yes, that's true. I never thought about it.' 'It was because they had been touched by sin that they were no longer innocent and their instincts could lead them to sin again.'

"Suddenly Luke ran off after a huge butterfly that had caught his eye. But as he was going he yelled back, as if to finish the conversation, 'Yes, yes, I really think I understand. Thanks Mom!'"

Talking about temptations and dangers that confront children, Paula R. mentioned something that seems very true.

"I have always tried to treat my children in a way that will enable them to feel my complete trust in them. At the same time, however, I have never tried to conceal either from myself or from them the continuous possibility we all have of falling and erring. Many times I have said to them, 'I know you wouldn't deliberately set out to do something wrong, but we mustn't forget our limitations. Whoever thinks, "I'm strong, therefore I can do this or that and it won't hurt me," had better watch out!' "

Purity means observing the order established by God

" 'What are impure acts?' Arthur asked me while I was helping him prepare for first communion," Mary S. related. "I explained how everything has been created by God for a purpose. Even the parts of the body, if each one is used according to God's intention, give him glory and everything is good and is in proper order and harmony. I also mentioned the book of Genesis, which says that after God created the various things he saw that they were good. If they are not used in the way he planned, there is disorder. 'The mouth,' I told him, 'for example, is for eating, the ears for hearing. But if we put peas in our ears, we are doing something which is disordered, senseless and unhealthy.

" 'So there are parts of the body that are very important, and these especially should not be used for things that are foolish, and dangerous. For example, the sacks that hold the seeds of a baby and the organ that is used to transport them. In fact, these seeds are very important, because when they meet the egg of the mother they bring new life to the world. For this reason, the organs that make them and carry them must be used only when one is an adult and married because that is how one becomes a father.' 'I understand, they are

needed by the wife,' he said very seriously and convinced. One of St. Paul's thoughts came immediately to
my mind. 'A woman no longer has dominion over her
body rather it belongs to her husband and likewise a
man is not master of his own body but his wife is.'

"Even though he asked me no more questions, I
was not exactly sure he had understood everything. But
one day, sometime later, he was downtown with my
husband and he saw some film advertisements which
were more or less obscene. Suddenly he put his thoughts
into words: 'Those pictures are just like impure acts.'
After a little more reflection he added, 'There are two of
my classmates who do certain things; when they grow
up they will be like the people in those pictures.' This
made it clear that he had nothing against his classmates,
but that he did understand and accurately condemned
what was wrong."

This concept of purity as the proper use of our
bodies and instincts according to God's plan came out
in almost all of our interviews. In light of this principle
parents have been able to confront and resolve many of
their children's earliest problems: tendencies to exhibit
oneself, to look at others, to touch oneself, innocent sex
play with others, masturbation and so on.

As Martha S. related: "One day Lucy confessed that
one of her friends would always lift up her skirt while
they were playing and she invited Lucy to do the same.
Naturally I did not scold her, but I realized that something needed to be said about purity. I tried to help her
understand that in our bodies we have a great gift, but
one that we must preserve till the proper time when it
is given in marriage, should that be our calling, since
that is why God has entrusted it to us. Another time,

Sam told me when he had returned from nursery school that he had undressed in front of a friend. I could tell by the way he spoke that his conscience was bothering him, warning him that something was not right. Therefore, without being hard on him, I explained that undressing in front of a friend or watching him do it might seem amusing, but I also explained to him the reasons why, in the natural order of things, it is better not to act that way."

Mary N. told us: "One morning during vacation, I had allowed Luke to stay in bed a while to look at the funnies in the newspaper because he had had a slight cold. When I entered his room to tell him to get up, I noticed that he had one hand inside his pajamas. At that moment I preferred to say nothing about it. But a couple of days later, while he was taking a bath, I said, "Luke, I want to tell you something. Sometimes in the morning when you wake up or when you are not quite awake, you may want to touch yourself because it feels good. At least, many children have that desire. However it is best not to do it, because that is such a delicate and important part of your body.' Since I had already explained fertilization to him, I was able to continue. 'In fact, that organ is used to give life and it must always be kept very clean so it stays healthy. You should not try to get pleasure from touching it, because that too is part of giving life and should wait for marriage when you want to become a father. Everything should be used for the purpose for which it was made. Otherwise there is disorder and this is not what God wants.' Luke became very serious, 'But I didn't know that!' he exclaimed. 'Now I will be careful. I didn't know it could be bad. But I have something else to tell you. Lots of times I have a dream that is very enjoyable. When I wake up, I do everything I can to go back to sleep and continue the dream. Sometimes I can, but if I can't I lie there and think about it, and I feel a nice tingling. I realize now that it is wrong to do that, isn't it?' I replied that dreams do not depend on our own will, but that thoughts do, so we should be careful about them. Since this conversation, my husband and I have tried to encourage him to get up as soon as he awakens."

Alice M. told us: "Our children, especially boys, should be told very early about the real significance of certain activities that they may innocently consider just fooling around. In almost every school—it seems incredible but it is true—there are boys who from first grade on invite others to share in this kind of behavior. My husband has taken care to spell out the dangers very clearly to our boys by telling them that this kind of activity is not according to God's plan.

Andrew M. had occasion to put his boys on guard against involvement with homosexuals. "Today, in church," said one of his boys, an eleven-year-old, "They read in St. Paul's Epistle that neither the immoral, nor thieves, nor homosexuals will enter the kingdom of heaven. What are homosexuals?" His father replied, "Physically, they are normal men or women; but unlike other men and women, they feel sexually attracted to people of their own sex." "Here I was able to explain," he continued, "how homosexual men sometimes seek the companionship of young boys. I also advised him to let me know if anyone, no matter who it may be, approaches him with unnatural familiarity, because this kind of behavior is against nature and against God who created it."

Christian marriage

The divinely established order leads also to the question of the spiritual values of marriage and the possibility of single people being 'givers of life.' These questions often arise even before we have had an opportunity to discuss fertilization with our children. Since they presume a religious or at least a moral vision of life they are among the most delicate questions we have to face.

" 'Do cats have to be married to have babies?', Louise asked me the other day after she had seen a cat feeding its kittens," Isabel C. related. "She was curious, I suppose, because I had just spoken with her about Christian marriage. 'A man and a woman,' I had told her, 'can have children,' and I meant this in a moral sense, 'only when they constitute a family before God.' I realized now that she had taken me literally. Therefore, I had to straighten things out and explain to her that cats do not have to marry, and neither do human beings, strictly speaking. They can have children without being married if they want to, but I went on to point out how many drawbacks this would have on the purely human and social level, not to mention the law of God and the importance of the sacramental grace of marriage."

"The last question that Larry asked me," Brian P. reported, "was: 'Can two people who are not married have children?' We had not yet discussed with him the role of the male in procreation, so I replied in this way, and it seemed to satisfy him: 'Think, for example about some of the people in the jungle. They love each other and they unite. They love each other so much that chil-

dren are born. However, they do not have the institu-
tion of marriage. Marriage is a sacrament instituted by
Jesus. But they do not know Jesus. They worship idols.
In Christianity, however, a woman and a man are united
not only because they love each other, but also because
they consider this union important from a religious
standpoint. Jesus himself calls them to form a family.'
From our conversation Larry was able to understand
that many people who are ignorant of the religious
aspect of the union can still have children without the
bond and the grace of the sacrament."

"As soon as I had finished explaining fertilization,"
Mary N. related to us, "Luke drew this conclusion:
'Then you can have children without being married.'
'Oh yes,' I replied. 'But if people are not married, God
will not send them children, will He?' 'God will allow
children to be born even to people who are not married.
If not, he would have to work against his own law of
nature. Now, I want to tell you something very difficult
to understand. Let's see if I can explain it well. It is very
important. A true union between a man and a woman
can come only from God, because only He, who is Love,
can succeed in making into one two human beings who
naturally incline toward selfishness.

" 'In Christian marriage, it is God himself who
unites husband and wife. For them to be united in every
sense, and not just physically, they have to have true
love, which means giving everything to the other person and forgetting oneself, losing everything for love, as
Jesus taught us on the cross.' I have never seen my son,
who tends to be somewhat superficial, more attentive or

touched than at that time. As though to himself, he commented, 'It seems very difficult, but it must be beautiful to be married like that.'"

Another beautiful but delicate experience is that of Esther G. with her eldest daughter.

"When Chris was in the hospital last year, she was thirteen. We have always been very sincere and open with each other, but had not yet discussed fertilization. At the hospital someone had given her the biography of Saint Maria Goretti, a well-written book, dramatic, but faithful to the truth. When I went to visit her, she told me about it with some agitation, and then asked me. 'But what was it that the boy wanted her to do? What did he want from her?' To tell the truth, I trembled at this moment because I had not yet had the chance to explain the process of fertilization to her; besides I was only with her a few hours every day and could not observe her reactions in case she needed help. I stopped a moment to gather my wits and ask Maria Goretti's help. I turned to my daughter and said: 'You must understand that men and women are physically different and that a mother and a father uniting together in marriage can produce new human beings. You, for example, were born because of the relationship of love between your father and myself. This is something very important and beautiful. The young man who loved Maria Goretti wanted to have with her this kind of life-producing relationship that exists between husband and wife. But before God this relationship is possible only in marriage. Outside marriage it is not according to the will of God. Maria Goretti did not want this sort of relationship, because she didn't want to depart from the will of God. She preferred to die rather than to submit to the man's request.'"

Dr. Andrew M. found it necessary to explain to his twelve-year-old daughter the substantial difference between the sexual act when it is carried out in marriage, and therefore according to the law and will of God, and when it is performed outside marriage.

"One day," he related to us, "while I was driving Ann to her aunt's for a visit, she complained about the fact that my wife and I did not like to let her go out alone. I had to explain the real dangers that exist, especially for a young girl who goes out unaccompanied. I warned her about the wiles and the deception of certain evil-minded men. Because I was driving the car, I was unable to see her immediate reaction. However, I could sense that she was listening attentively. 'But why do they do that?' she asked me. I talked about the desires of these men and what they were looking for, that is, simply sexual relations. But here I took special care not to disturb her or put marital relations in a negative light. I said, 'So you see, even though what I am describing may seem crude to you, it is the best way to warn you about the dangers a young girl might face. In marriage, on the other hand, the physical manifestation of love and the union of two people is very beautiful, wonderful, and blessed by God. It is a very worthy thing because it can be the start of a new life.'

"So it happened in an unexpected and spontaneous way that I was able to instill moral values. This led to a good discussion of virginity, not only as an anatomical fact but also as an important religious and moral basis for living.

"There are people," commented Dr. M., after having related this episode, "who maintain that while masturbation is psychologically negative because it leaves a sense of degradation and failure, pre-marital sex relations are positive because they give a feeling of strength and success and help to avoid many neuroses. Here I must say, to put it ridiculously, that if one had to be neurotic to be Christian, then I would want to be neurotic and want all my children to be that way as well. However, in actual fact Jesus, as man and God, has given us even from a human point of view the best principles for our full, complete and harmonious development as human beings."

CONCLUSION

We have now covered all the subjects dealt with in our interviews. As you can easily see, we have not made mention of the deviations, deformations and more serious sexual aberrations, which are, sad to say, more common that many realize. These subjects simply did not come up during our interviews and, since they belong to the field of pathology, are better left to physicians and psychiatrists.

The fact remains that even with perfectly normal children, we continuously make many mistakes while carrying out our responsibilities as educators.

Sometimes these errors can be of little consequence, other times so grave that they seem irreparable, still other times we are absolutely sure we have completely failed and totally ruined everything in our efforts at educating our children. Never, however, can we allow ourselves to be overcome by discouragement or by desperation. Even our mistakes, once we realize them, can be turned to good, insofar as they bring us to adjust our positions and our methods.

Besides, parents who are serious about Christian

education must be determined that whenever they admit defeat, if they place themselves in his hands, God the Father will intervene to fill every void, heal every wound, and "make all things new." As many of those we interviewed have told us, our children are more his than ours and, as a result, they are even dearer to him, than to us.

Andrew M. concluded his interview with a reference to Christian parents: "We have an advantage over many other parents, because we know that we are not alone. Whatever we do not succeed in accomplishing ourselves will be done by Someone else."